I0749561

BOOK CLUB BOOK

BOOK CLUB BOOK

REGINA AGU

NATHANIEL DONNETT

QUINCY FLOWERS

EGIE IGHILE

STEFFANI JEMISON

OTABENGA JONES & ASSOCIATES

AYANNA JOLIVET MCCLOUD

MICHAEL KAHLIL TAYLOR

TABLE OF CONTENTS

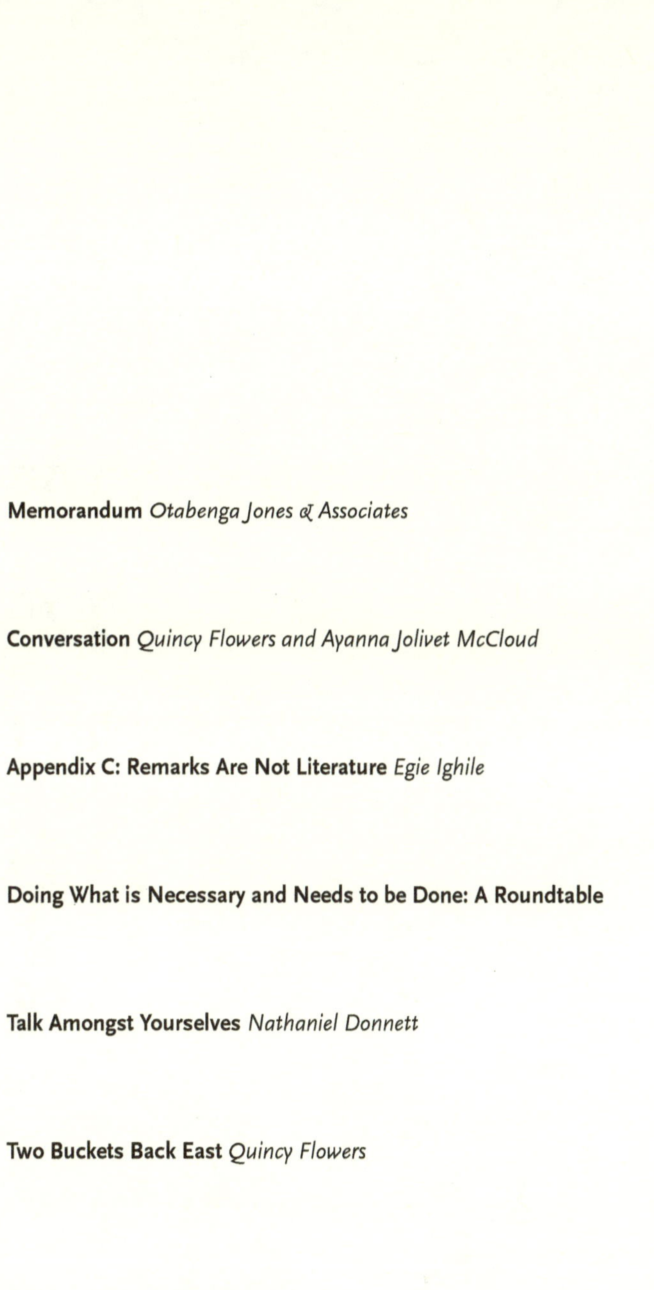

Something real—in that it might have been otherwise—happened.

—Fred Moten

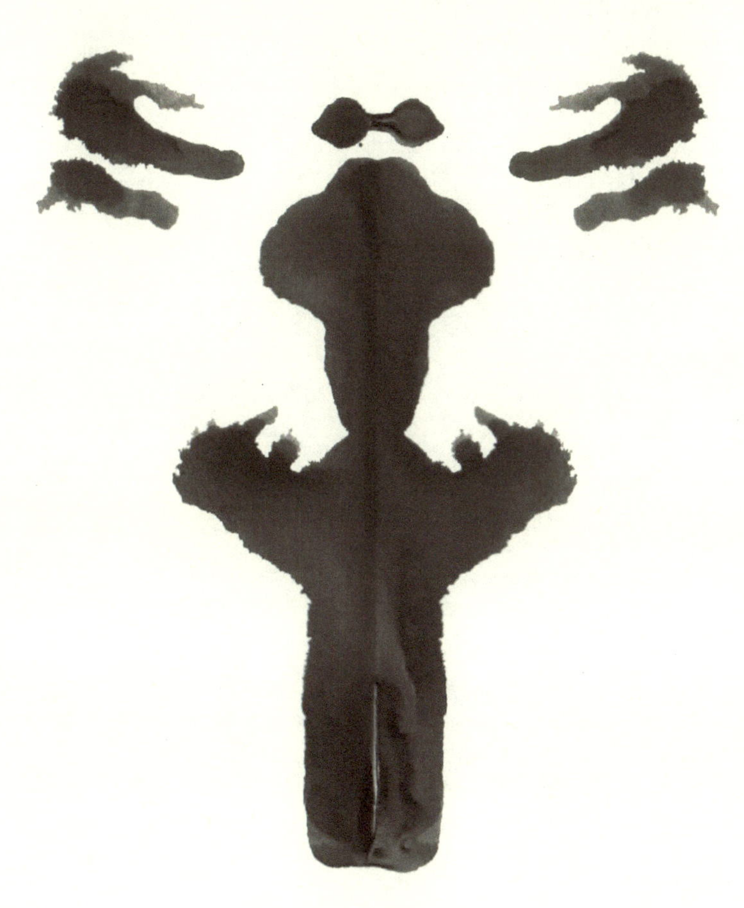

MEMORANDUM

Otabenga Jones & Associates

The 1960's saw a surge of creative activity in the world of advertising. Looking for an effective means to spread the messages of Black consciousness existing at that time, activist/artist Otabenga Jones saw an opening in advertising to affect the hearts and minds of the American public. After a run-in with marketing guru George Lois on a basketball court in the Lower East Side, Jones began interning at the newly formed ad agency Lois Holland & Callaway. He spent three valuable years at that agency learning the intricacies of mass communication, eventually leaving New York City for Chicago to join the Black-owned Vince Cullers Advertising Inc. There, he found an excellent opportunity to speak to a Black audience, utilizing training he had gained at the Lois agency as well as ideas he had developed on his own. However, his time in Chicago was short-lived. After eight months with Cullers, Jones was let go after refusing to develop a campaign aimed at Black consumers for the Oscar Mayer corporation. Although his professional ambitions were unfulfilled (certain incompatibilities with the corporate mindset are evident in his first memorandum), the time spent with the agency allowed him to codify strategies for communicating in multi-voiced, and often hostile environments. These strategies were centered around a characteristic of Black Expression termed "angularity," which he would also use while working as a writer for the NBC sitcom Sanford and Son. The following is a memo Mr. Jones wrote to his creative team upon arrival to the Cullers Agency, explaining his creative influences and agenda.

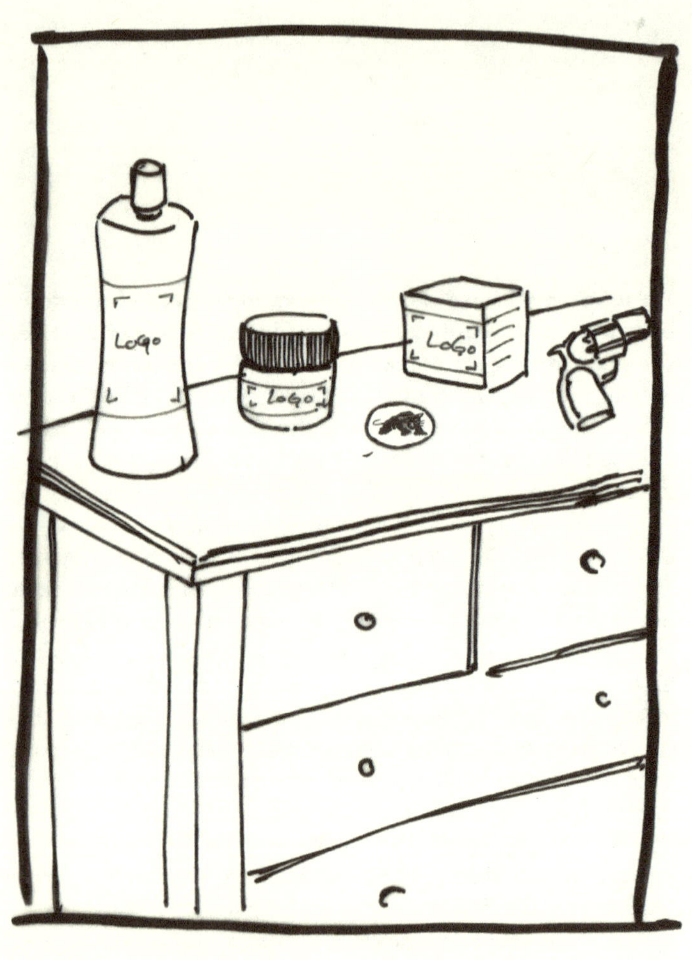
LoGo
LoGo
LoGo

INTEROFFICE MEMORANDUM

To: ________________________ Date: 8/1/66
____
____

Habari gani,

It is with great pleasure that I now count myself amongst the staff of this organization! I am looking forward to working with you, my sisters and brothers in the struggle, towards the creative growth I see awaiting us on the horizon. My reason for penning this memo is not to introduce myself. The time we will spend together during the next few weeks developing our first ad campaign will provide ample opportunity for us to get acquainted. My reason for penning this memo is to share with you, as creative director, the types of communication strategies I believe will allow us to enter the psyches of our markets, and to win the battles of persuasion that have been engaged all over this country and beyond.

But before proceeding I must say that in my opinion, our ultimate goal in crafting ads is not merely to sell products, though we can do that. As far as I am concerned the world needs only one type of car, one type of shoe, television, typewriter, etc. The goal of our practice is to use the conduits of mass media to extend mantras, both verbal and visual, that increase the intensity of the light of Blak consciousness we now see dawning. On this journey we will undoubtedly meet resistance, which we can withstand, but only as a unified front.

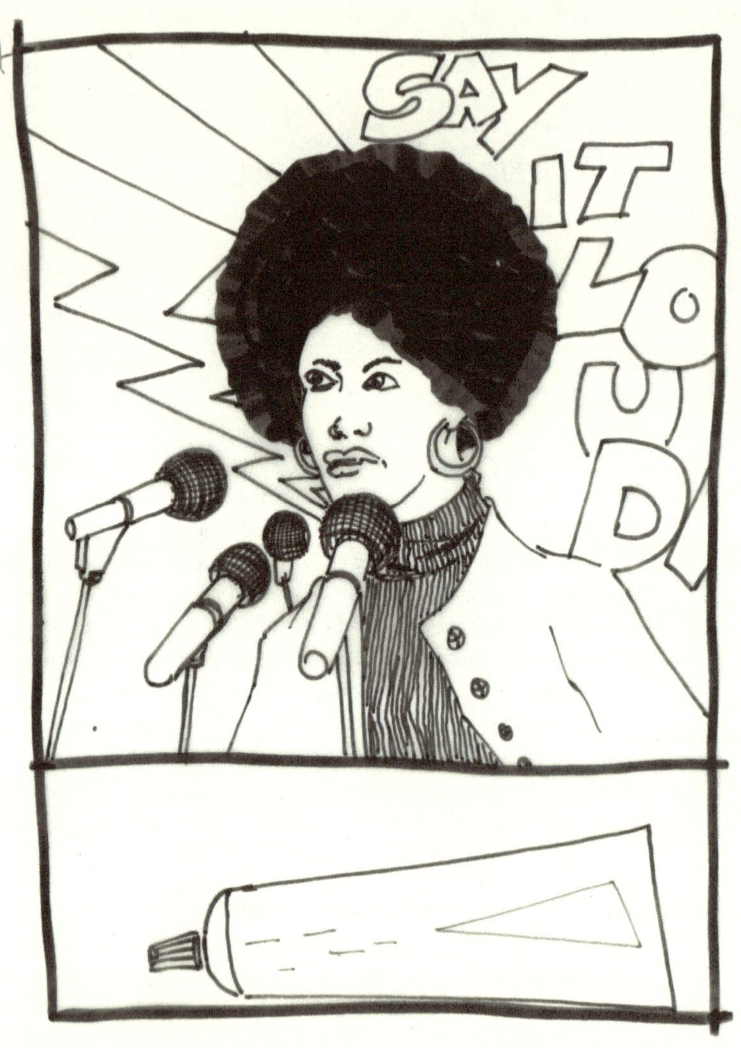
SAY IT LOUD

There exists at our disposal a method of subversive communication developed over centuries by African and African American scientists. This method came into fruition in an environment more hostile than our own, where particular sentiments had to be concealed. Despite these conditions, coded messages were transmitted. The messages remained elusive to those who were not intended to receive them, proving the strategies effective. I feel wholeheartedly that this method will work for us, too, in this new arena.

Though there is historical data relating to the above method, chronicled in slave narratives and folktales, I have relied heavily upon what anthropologist and novelist Zora Neale Hurston in her essay "Characteristics of Negro Expression"* has labeled "angularity." We will approach "angularity" as a formal and conceptual device, reflecting some of the basic needs and desires of Black life. It is our job to take it apart, put it back together, and decide how we will use it.

BASIC TENETS

Angles signify: Time, Direction, Motion, Vitality
Angles have the ability to make covert, and to confuse.
"Hittin' a lick with a crooked stick"
We will make these tenets the foundation of our communication style.

Copywriters (consider the use of)

Alliteration
Analogy
Verbal nouns
Metaphor
Onomatopoeia

Designers (consider the use of)

Actual and implied angles/diagonals
Complementary and Triadic color harmonies
Sequential imagery

---

* Hurston, Zora Neale. "Characteristics of Negro Expression" Hurston, and Wall. *Sweat.* New Brunswick, N.J.: Rutgers University Press, 1997. 55–72

Dynamic postures and gestures
Text styles appropriate for such moods

By next week check out
The Collected Stories of Joel Chandler Harris (Brer Rabbit is extremely angular in his logic)
The works of Thelonious Monk (just for names' sake lets start with *Brilliant Corners*)
John Gilmore's work with the Jazz Messengers (for the adventurous check out his work with the Sun Ra Arkestra)
Alabama slave quilts

*We will discuss these concepts further in our breakout session on Wednesday the 11th. I am very interested in hearing how you think these ideas can be utilized in the new P&G beauty campaign.

Free the land,

Otabenga Jones

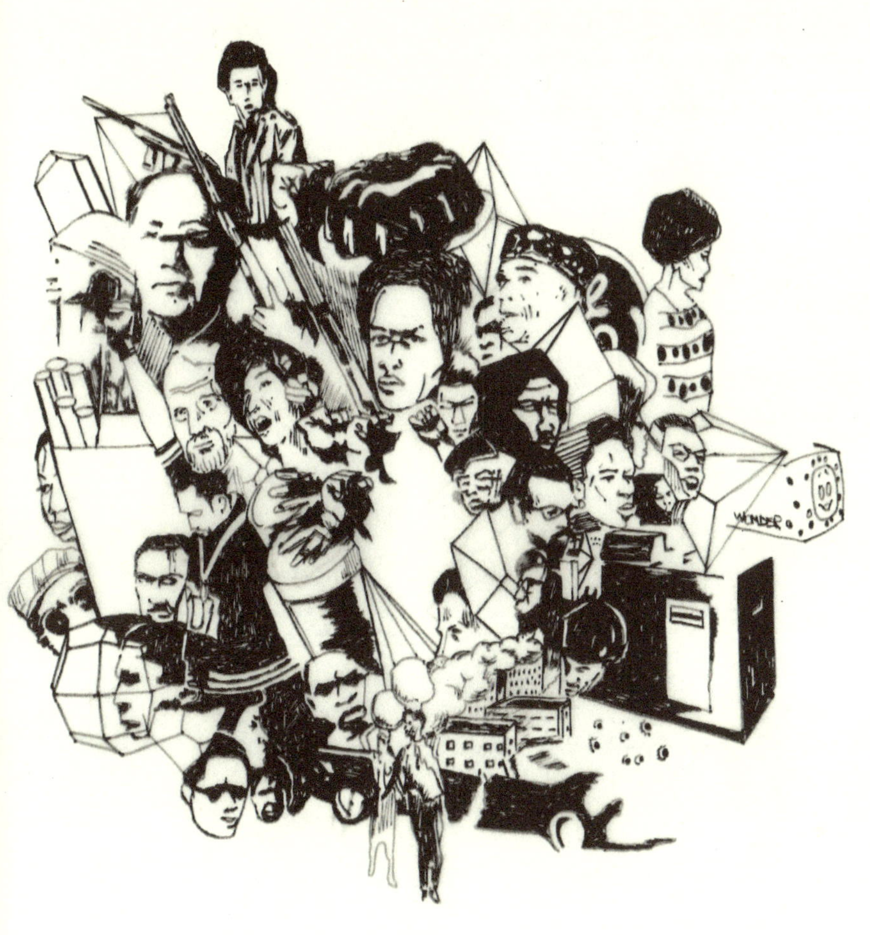
WONDER

CONVERSATION

Quincy Flowers and Ayanna Jolivet McCloud

Transcript of conversation:

Quincy Flowers and Ayanna Jolivet Mccloud
12/10/10 1:00pm
2316 Elgin, Houston, Texas

Ayanna: Often times, I connect with [black people]. There is a certain language that can take place without us even talking. And I'm not necessarily talking about eye contact...our experiences are far-ranging, but there are certain rhythms. Aligning ourselves on the basis of blackness sort of weighs us down. But it's powerful too.

Quincy: I can put a million black people in a room and we have this way to relate. Is that because we been paying attention—because of the [nineteen] sixties, fifties, forties, thirties, twenties expressions of blackness, you know what I mean? We've been paying attention to that medium. Blackness has been producing the things we've always been paying attention to—all of us. And we just as well could have been paying attention to any other performances out there in the world (and probably have).

But what happens when I unplug? What happens when I unplug from those narratives? And I don't want to have anything to do with them and I'm like you know what I'm going to go into, all my art, I'm basing it off Greek tropes. Forget this black language, and I've read all of the Harlem Renaissance stuff and I don't want to hear it listen to it read it anymore. From here on out, if you don't know anything about Greek mythology you will not understand [the work of Quincy Flowers]. Will the black organization for black artists still invite me to the party? Or did I lose my black card? You know what I mean—I'm interested in that. You know—what is blackness? Is it just being black? Does it have black politics? What is it? When we put these people in a room and we have to have a discussion, on what basis do we do it? You know what I mean?

That [scenario] is not farfetched. It's farfetched for me because I haven't done that with my life, but I can almost definitely say that there is someone out there who is not recognized as a black person anymore by his black people.

[*Laughter*]

So is blackness dated?

Ayanna: I think it is. You know, I don't know that I would say...[*laugh*] This is funny because I feel like you're saying some things that are kind of similar to me but it's not exactly similar. There are these parallels. How does one perceive blackness? Black people and non-black people—how we perceive blackness has to be resisted. The problem is that often because of the blackness will not allow us to penetrate all of our other identities.

Quincy: Say that again: Through the blackness....

Ayanna: Because of the blackness

Quincy: Because of the blackness

Ayanna: Because of the blackness...so for me...let's say I'm a black woman with multiple identities. I feel like I have this working class background, the way I identify with my sexuality is far-ranging. It's not always—you know, it's not so straight. But there's not much room for [multiplicity]...you know, if I'm in a black...

Quincy: Exactly.

Ayanna: I'm black. And it is assumed that I am this way this way and this way. Like we all have this history. As soon as I walk through that door and I'm black, that overshadows everything else. You know? I feel like it's very unique compared to other groups.

Quincy: You think so? I don't know. I think anytime you put multiple people together to represent an identity, they have to chop off the other parts of them[selves] to even form a group. I think white men in a group lose a part of themselves by identifying as "white men." There are all kind of ways that they are different—he's "the white man married to the black girl." He's "the white man who is gay." There are all different kinds of "white men," but if they walk into the room and have a "white man" meeting ... they lose as much of themselves as we lose of ourselves.

Ayanna: I think it is an American thing where race overshadows everything. I don't know other examples but it is true—it's not just a black thing. But ... I do feel within the black community there is a lot of weight. Like this fighting that we've been doing ... I question all of this fighting that we've been doing. There's always this language of fighting.

Quincy: Who's fighting?

Ayanna: Black people to move forward. You know, like progress. We are fighting to create progress and move forward.

Quincy: We're soldiers. [*laughing*]

Ayanna: [*not laughing*] Yeah, we're soldiers. There are many of us who are fighting to provide, you know, just to stay alive. That's a class thing but it is a black thing too.

Quincy: You know, the conversations we been having in Book Club, I wouldn't mind having them with every single population. I think the concerns I have and those that came up in the group, they're not black problems to me. You know what I mean? They're white man's problems. They're women problems. They're you-just-got-off-the-plane-and-now-you-live-here problems. They're so important for everybody to recognize. And I think that that's the new ... if I'm thinking about a 2011 version of blackness, I think it's that. And it's not even new. The sixties were doing that. The League of Revolutionary Black Workers that I'm studying right now, they did that. They were like, "No, white man. I would love to have you work with our organization, but politically, we need a group of all black people and you need to go and organize the white men in the factory. I'm not saying that our struggle is not your struggle." They were saying some very profound, very progressive things back then. And the fact that they won't teach white kids this ... that's ... that's ... I don't like that. Why is that only a lesson for me to know? I'm a black boy so they are like, "Hey, did you read this?" I got to read about my history. But the little white boy, no one ever tells him, "Yo, you want to know your history? Well you need to read about the Black Revolutionary Workers." I think everybody needs to know about the League of Revolutionary Black Workers. Because then we would know that the people were concerned with the system....

I'm not interested in getting together with just black people. We had Book Club, and I think that it was great that nobody else was invited. But I don't think that what we talked about is only for our ears.

Notes written from above conversation:

what is blackness? is blackness dated?

the conversation is often being done by the people doing the ????

letting that group have agency for themselves and inviting them to the conversation.

what is the conversation about? who is it to benefit?

trauma/to help people heal ... skeptical of helping heal.

structure...

dated model ... give birth to something brand new

when you get to a place where you lose the structure and lose the form is it blackness that's still standing?

aligning ourselves on that basis on blackness, does that keep us chained to...

against homogeneity ... in 2010 it's so complicated ... we're going to be pulled together by our black selves ... ignores the deeper problematic, want even about the place

a complete narrative ... what's beyond that ... an oppressive force ... the problem of slavery being day one/starting point of our history/narrative

the conversations we're having are not black people's problems

race was/is abstract

what happens when we unplug from those narratives

rewriting history/future

nonresistant

ironies/ losing structures

paradox

the role of imagination

new space

dominance of blackness

how do we do something that's not old fashioned

the need to hit the reset button

– As Artists –

Name & things –
- blackness –
- crises
- then / us –
-

New Structures
- new language –
- new actions

Lose structure + history etc. is blackness still standing

– Organically.

Is black politics relevant today?

– blackness – dated –
– black is dominant trait –

– Process –

7–10 – questions –

- email notes
- email questions – 10 questions
- answer 7 questions – answer
- another layer of response

QUESTIONS (FOR AYANNA FROM QUINCY)

1. *You discuss "healing" and "purging" in regards to what needs to occur in the black community. Can you tell me what you mean by this?*

I'm particularly interested in purging. I think purging is an action that often gets left out of the conversation when it comes to talking about community building, let alone the black community. I know purging sounds a bit undesirable. When you look it up in the dictionary, one of the definitions for it is "to rid of impurities." I see purging as simply getting it all out, with no filters. Before we can talk about solutions and next steps, I think it's necessary to simply sit still and to talk, and to listen. Through different political movements and various pedagogies, I believe we've got a certain way of discussing blackness. It is often rooted in practicalities and tangible solutions, and sometimes becomes a bit didactic, that I'm interested in purging as functioning as a kind of purgatory, an in-between state, with no judgment, no movement, which is somewhat meditative. I'm interested in this blank slate. I think it might reinvigorate the dialogue.

2. *I thought a lot about your contributions in Book Club discussions regarding the idea of organic movement. Referring to past actions, you describe different moments—when people got together in a collaborative effort to organize social or art movements—as happening organically. You suggest that each situation presented opportunities (if you will allow me to say that) to motivate people to plan and act according a shared agenda. Is something happening like that now? Is there in our midst or somewhere close ahead this kind of opportunity for people to come together in a way we haven't seen since the 60s? I'm thinking again about the purging you speak about because you seem to do so in a way that suggests that this healing is approaching.*

In Book Club meetings we discussed organic movement in contrast to organized movement. I was probably one to really embrace organic movement. I think that before organized movement occurs there has to be an impetus, which is what organic movement is all about. Organic movement provides a foundation for organized movement. Presently, I don't know if there is any kind of parallel movement leading to something similar to the Civil Rights Movement, and to tell you the truth I don't know if it will happen in such a concentrated, momentous way.

It might be something where numerous small movements arise, you know small reverberations.

5. *Has Book Club changed the way you think about your work?*

It has reminded me of the complexities of blackness, as well as the contradictions of it. It has introduced to me to some very interesting and progressive writing and voices, which has inspired and reminded me that these independent, subversive, avant-garde, and plural voices have always existed within the black community. I really connect with some of the authors and I am also affirmed that blackness is not singular. It has not changed how I think about my artwork, but maybe how I think about my art practice.

Questions (for Quincy from Ayanna):

4. *In our conversations at Book Club you stated that in talking about Black people that rather than beginning at a "fix it" attitude, you're interested in "using it". Often times we hear so many people talking for working class and working-poor Black folks. You've discussed that we need let these people "have agency for themselves" and we also may learn something from them instead of expecting them to learn something from others. I agree and believe that a lot of my own experience has been informed by "using it" and also this "magic" you mentioned to. I'm wondering what are some things you think we learn if we let them "having agency for themselves"?*

I am not a good member of any collective that purports to amalgamate multiple concerns under the umbrella of a unified goal, when a decision must be made about the form and direction of a project, which has everything to do with deciding on explicit goals while rejecting others. There is no possibility of a collective center since any competing goals must be resolved into one goal. And I am too selfish for that.

This limits my engagement in traditional politics. I became an artist because I do not like to be bound by practical concerns. I don't like having to make sense of everything, to find reasons and allow them to guide my decisions. It gets to be loud. But I do not have to prioritize my thoughts in that way; as an artist I have the freedom to go wherever I want to go. I'm also saying that many, many others out there in the world, without becoming artists, have found ways to go wherever they want to go too.

7. Has Book Club changed the way you think about your work? If so, how?

For one thing, I had always envied visual artists. As a writer, I was limited by the American English words I knew, and the conventions associated with them. When I looked at visual art works, they were so far removed from a bounded book or literary journal that the main thing I saw was the artists' lack of boundaries. So to hear visual artists expressing similar restrictions surrounding their practice and the art world in general was kind of perplexing.

Book Club has allowed me to hear the ways in which any black artist in an American context faces particular expectations that are not very different from what writers deal with. You know, as far as art and writing are concerned, there is a 1950s mentality regarding what people choose to view: these artists are for black people and this one is for women and things like that. No one says it outright anymore. But if you ask someone what artists or writers she knows, it is extremely likely that her demographic membership will coincide with her reading habits.

I had already been thinking about much of this in terms of letters, but Book Club gave the situation more depth. It has inspired me to think more urgently about resisting those expectant beings whose expectations are drawn heavily from my identity as a black man.

APPENDIX C:
REMARKS ARE NOT LITERATURE

Egie Ighile

(Facebook message from Egie Ighile to Steffani Jemison on November 21, 2010 at 8:35 pm)

I enjoyed taking part in the book club tonight. It was good to have that kind of conversation. If you'll indulge me for a minute, I want to elaborate on a point I made during the discussion, in hope of clarifying the point of view for which I was arguing at the time. When the discussion turned to the reasons for which artists come together, seek "solidarity" etc. it seemed the general point of view expressed in the room was that it is always done in reaction to things that are taking place within the culture at large. And in attempting to argue for a different way of seeing things, I made reference to a number of artistic movements, but failed to make my case. Finally, I made mention of Picasso and Braque and their joint creation of Cubism, but I think what I was trying to bring to light with that example still wasn't clear.

I think the general point of view is right: all creation takes place in a context; that context being the thing towards which the artist reacts. But this inevitability of the reactive impulse doesn't necessarily determine how an artist reacts (or even to what part of the culture he or she chooses to react primarily). With Picasso and Braque, keeping to that example, the pertinent question would be why was it Picasso and Braque who invented Cubism, and not, say, Matisse and Derain? Why

Cubism as a result of those two particular individuals, and not two others? My point being that what brought Picasso and Braque together was an aesthetic sensibility shared by two individuals, a shared way of seeing, artistically speaking, a shared perception of reality and of how to reshape that reality on a canvas.

This, of course, relates to my point—and the point Ayanna made—about "blackness" over-determining the aesthetic stance of the "black" artist. (I put the word in scare quotes to highlight the abstract nature of the term.) Don't get me wrong, I am not against black solidarity, and I think it has its place in the arts as a necessary corrective to hegemonic discourse and institutions, but I do think that as artists we should be able to maintain that space that allows for the individual development of aesthetic stance. To be stamped into a monolithic mold of being is its own form of oppression. The politics of "blackness" and the aesthetics of "blackness" do not necessarily refer to the same definition of "blackness."

My personal point of view (which others may disagree with, hence its being personal) is that political "blackness" is a largely instrumentalized "blackness" i.e "blackness" put toward a pragmatic (read: socio-economic) end, but aesthetic "blackness" resides in whatever work of aesthetic value (and values are subjective) a "black" person creates; how others then choose to see that creation is, as far I am concerned, their own business.

• • •

[bookclubx] Some thoughts on yesterday's reading

Monday, December 20, 2010 2:34 PM
From: "egie ighile" <XXXXXX@XXXXX>
To: xbookclubx@XXXXXXXX

I'm rereading the essay "Beyond Black Representational Space,"* the text requiring rumination. Here are a few notes commenting on the first paragraph that I hope clarify the thrust of my argument from

* English, Darby. "Beyond Black Representational Space" in *How to See a Work of Art in Total Darkness*. Cambridge, Mass: MIT Press, 2007. 1–26

yesterday. Like I said, I find the essay rather ironic. Hopefully, I offend no one with my polemics. Quotations are in italics.

"What becomes of black art when black people stop making it?"

So long as there are black people there will always be black art, black art defined as art made by people socially constructed as "black." For the artist, the designation "black art" need have no further bearing beyond that. If critics and historians want to wrestle with the tar-baby, that's their problem. I use the term "tar-baby" to indicate that, from the artist's point of view, the term "black art" is only a problem if one makes it a problem. The sticky nature of the term can in fact become arsenal for the cunning artist.

"These artists do not endeavor simply to do more than just race work with their art, but precisely to be seen as doing so"

This implicitly shortchanges black art (i.e. art made by people socially constructed as black). The default of black art is (dismissed as?) race work. What the fuck is race work? Work that self-consciously attempts to uplift the race, yeah? Shall we then assume that black signifiers + transcendence = race work? Keep in mind that the quest for transcendence has a long history in Western art going back to at least Plato. Are the idealized forms of ancient Greece and the Italian renaissance white race work? Are the Benin & Ife bronzes race work? How about Aaron Douglas, Romare Bearden, Henry Ossawa Tanner—race work?

Or is race work simply work that has black signifiers, period? In which case, if you wanna make "art" beyond "race work" then you better scrub your work clean of that shit (or at least "be seen" in some way as doing so).

All of which raises the question of what is a black signifier? The black body, of course, is the black signifier par excellence. (Combine the idea in that last sentence with the idea in the paragraph above and one reaches the conclusion that we are part of the shit we need to scrub out of our own work in order to make "art." Now that's a pleasant thought.) How about abstraction? Is that a black signifier? Keep in mind the long history of abstraction in art made by those socially constructed as black.

Or does black art, being race work, we are told, by definition entail a literalizing of representation?

"One of my objectives here is to underscore the loses entailed by mistaking the appreciably black spirit of this art for a wholesale enlistment in a category that would become its only context."

My point is that this is nothing new. Neither critic nor artist is engaged in anything new. (And funny how the argument moves from "black art" to "black spirit,"—spooks, huh?) This mode of appreciation should be applied to the entire history of "black art" (once again, defined as art made by people socially constructed as black, whether now or in the past—keeping in mind the historicity of the term "black"). And by not doing so (*"What becomes of black art when black artists stop making it?"*) he gets tangled up in the tar-baby. If I take a Dogon mask and can only explicate it under the rubric of "black art" then that speaks of my own myopic understanding of the work. It is no commentary on the vision of the Dogon sculptor that made it.

• • •

Re: [bookclubx] Charles Gaines, *Art Lies* and Metaphor and Metonymy

Thursday, December 23, 2010 11:41 PM
From: "egie ighile" <XXXXXX@XXXXX>
To: xbookclubx@XXXXXXXX

Okay, I read the essay,* and in lieu of a counter-essay (ain't got the time for that joint) here are a few remarks:

Heaven help us when Mr. Dubya Malaprop aka George Bush becomes the lodestone of our language.

That water can be used as an instrument of political oppression doesn't mean that water is inherently sinister. Make una ask Fela Kuti; he go tell una water no get enemy. No different with metaphor. And, yeah, I just used a metaphor—so sue me. These guys talk a

* Gaines, Charles. "Reconsidering Metaphor/Metonymy: Art and the Suppression of Thought." *Art Lies* 64 (Winter 2009). 48–57

good game, but I ain't buying what they're selling. Oops! Another metaphor. How sinister of me.

They want to deconstruct the apparatus of language to hip us to its built-in semiotics of oppression. Good luck with that, fellas. How noble. How proper. Never mind that to make their argument against metaphor they are forced to use metaphors.

Gillick's observation raised the unsettling possibility that a trope that has been considered central to our very idea of what it means to be human and which has its noblest expression in works of art can be used as an instrument of repression.

The word "central" in the paragraph above, which points out metaphor as the accused in this criminal investigation, is itself a metaphor. "Central" means "pertaining to the center." And here is the etymology of word "center"—late 14c., from O.Fr. centre (14c.), from L. centrum "center," originally fixed point of the two points of a compass, from Gk. kentron "sharp point, goad, sting of a wasp,"—so in tracing the word's meaning we go from the sting of a wasp to the fixed point of a compass used to diagram space, leading to a further leap from the spatial to the abstract which finally enables us to speak of a trope being central to an idea. So I ask: what does it mean for anything to be "central" to an idea? Is an idea an object in space that it can be said to have a center?

In like manner, one can go through the entire essay picking out the words used metaphorically or, to be more accurate, picking out metaphors we have accustomed into literalness: *raised, unsettling, formed, illumination, mapping, transfer, structure* ... but that would get tedious. Once done, there would be no essay left.

Metaphor is a trope or figure where two unrelated signs are mapped together based on some similarity or analogy between them ... Meaning, therefore, plays no role in how metaphors are formed

This makes no sense to me. Similarity and analogy are means of constructing meaning. Indeed I would further argue that perceptive metaphors reveal relations. The universe is not a bundle of disjointed bits and pieces; interrelation is the nature of reality, or rather I should say that interrelation is the inevitable nature of our perception of reality

Take the example: "John is a wolf." The signs "John" and "wolf," two completely unrelated ideas, are being compared.

This example is as weak as an arthritic knee. "Two unrelated ideas," really? I guess the fact that both John and the wolf are animals and thanks to nature share certain aspects of animal psychology including aggression doesn't really count as a relation. The elided truth here (which the author in fact doesn't mention) that wolves are actually less aggressive than humans isn't metaphor's fault but the fault of the men who made cliché of this particular metaphor and subsequently ceased to pay attention to actual wolves. How about if I said instead "John is a carburetor." What could I mean by that? What greater truth am I eliding thereby? John and the carburetor do seem to be way more unrelated than John and the wolf. Surely I have some subterfuge up my sleeve. But this expression too could be made clear if the context in which it was used *highlighted the nature of the relation* being made and thereby imbued the expression with meaning.

I am proposing that metaphoric thinking is not critical thinking.

I am proposing that the above proposition is hogwash.

All figurative language—metonymy (the hero to metaphor's villain in our scholars' telling of the tale), synecdoche, irony, and the whole host of other rhetorical devices besides—all language, period—can be used to occlude critical thinking. Take this sentence:

"The White House believes a healthy Wall Street means a healthy Main Street."

That's all metonymy with no metaphors in sight. But what is it really saying? Do you get any sense of largely self-interested collusion between our elected leaders and the country's financial elite that a sentence such as the above usually serves as justification for? It sounds like the kind of language the media and government routinely deploy to pull the wool over our eyes. Am I now to bring a legal brief against metonymy because of the possible uses to which it can be put? Orwell's essay "Politics and the English language" is, of course, the classic dissection of this form of rhetorical crime.

A metonym is the relationship or coming together of two signs based upon contiguity, that is, social agreement, and not a similarity between them.

"Social agreement"? Every act of establishing meaning in language is an act of social agreement. Metonymy is not unique in this. Some figures of speech simply become so common that their meanings appear to be transparent. We no longer think about them. One of the things good prose tries to do is unsettle this contentment with apparent transparency and jog the mind into thought through fresh language.

There's more to be said about all this but I think I'll chill for now.

I am left wondering, though, how these scholars' (faulty) thesis about language is meant to serve as foundation for a theory of the visual arts.

• • •

Re: [bookclubx] podcast

Tuesday, January 18, 2011 2:09 AM
From: "egie ighile" <XXXXXX@XXXXX>
To: xbookclubx@XXXXXXXX

I think the anecdote about your white friend <a writer> who is envious of "oppressed" people is rather funny. Hilarious, in fact. That's a potentially rich premise for a story. I have often thought it quite ironic how conflict is narrative's reason for being—it needs conflict, it is fed and nourished by conflict—and yet conflict is the very condition narrative ever tries to get beyond through resolution, catharsis, self-purgation etc. The nature of narrative is a quixotic quest (or perhaps a Faustian bargain) to get beyond its own being. A story is an argument against itself, against that very thing which makes it possible. Perhaps an appropriate metaphor for the human condition.

I can't co-sign the scholar's thesis* about what defines the body of work we call African-American literature, but it is a truism that

---

* Warren, Kenneth W. "Does African-American Literature Exist?" The Chronicle of Higher Education (February 24, 2011).
http://chronicle.com/article/Does-African-American/126483/

African-American writers have labored under a greater burden of representation than other American writers have.

My view of literature tends toward abstraction. Stories beget stories, books beget books, poems beget poems. I would echo the Roman playwright, Terence and say (appropriated cliché though it may be) that I consider nothing that is human alien to me. Terence was the originator of the Roman stage trope of "contamination" in which characters from multiple Greek plays were appropriated and brought together in a single new Roman play which re-imagined the identities of these originally Greek characters. I would say that there is a sense in which the whole of literature can be thought of as a vast storehouse of contaminations which create the possibility for further contaminations. This was actually going to be the springboard for my bookclub essay before it got rudely hijacked by a poem.

I don't consider any book to be written for me and yet I consider every book to be written for me. I take from each what I will...or I don't. Who is this "me" I go on talking about, anyway? And what business do words have in defining me? what business do narratives?

I have little patience for anything that would presume to define me and my concerns which doesn't first address what makes me me. Once one starts from that premise with regard to any person—the premise of the elusiveness of self—then the really interesting discussion begins, a discussion to which we are yet to find bottom....

Every identity is a construct.

I would like to swallow the whole bloody storehouse of literature, as much of it as I can, from Gilgamesh to present day, ranging across as many cultures as I can contaminate my wayward brain with, and with that proceed to ventriloquize new contaminations. I believe one has authority for whatever stories one can tell well. (and there is a lot contained in that word "well.")

How all this relates to how works of literature are received is another issue. As stated during our discussion, my view on this is largely intransigent. The struggle to write and then write well is hard enough.

If I am able to create what I set out to create, that is triumph already. If it speaks to only a few, I have no problem with that.

As for strategy, with Objectif I choose in a manner of speaking to play the culture game. I use that as hedge to get me by while I take my good time and tinker on this other shit (who knows for how long?) which in the end only a smattering, if any, may give a shit about.

• • •

Re: [bookclubx] podcast

Tuesday, January 18, 2011 11:31 AM
From: "egie ighile" <XXXXXX@XXXXX>
To: xbookclubx@XXXXXXXX

To answer Nathaniel's question:

My theory is that black literature stands in different relation to literary culture and the history of literature than relation between black music and the history of music.

Music and literature operate differently. The interplay between form and content in each art form is different. Arthur Jafa in his essay "My Black Death"* talks about how music can travel disembodied from its maker or even the *image* of its maker. In music, form can completely subsume content. The art form is an interrelation of sounds, vibrations of air which need denote nothing ... and can connote everything.

Africans in America infused new vibrations into the sound of Western music, new rhythms, new chords, new timbres. Some of these sounds were associated with narratives (blues), some weren't (jazz). My point is that the sounds could be abstracted from the narratives and appropriated and transformed (for instance, the history of how black rock n' roll morphs into white rock).

---

* Jafa, Arthur. "My Black Death" in *Everything but the Burden: What White People Are Taking from Black Culture*. G. Tate, ed. New York: Broadway Books, 2003. 244–57

With literature, though it too begins with sound, words by their nature denote. There must be a signified for every signifier. Words and combinations of words create connotations, but the denotative is always there and creates lesser or greater imaginative tensions. So, literature is read for the images it creates, the narratives it conveys. And though one can speak of the "musicality" of language, one can't entirely abstract the form from its content. (Ambitious poets have tried). Nathanael Mackey's essay about "othering"* was an attempt to bring attention to formal elements of black literature by centering upon the idiolect of black speech and how black literary artists manipulate this.

The thing about "black speech" (used here as a metaphor for all "black" literature) is that it presumes a black speaker, a black narrator. This narrator is in fact the content of the work. A white writer who wants to write "black" literature is therefore obliged to don a black mask, unlike music where the sounds, depending on the degree to which one manipulates them purely as sound, can be abstracted from their black origin, their black image.

William Styron's *The Confessions of Nat Turner*** is an example of a work by a white writer that attempts to speak through the consciousness of a black protagonist. Upon release, it caused much controversy. I haven't read the book, so I can't proffer an opinion as to its success or failure. I'm will say that I'm not against a white writer writing such a book on principle any more than I'm against a black writer inhabiting a white protagonist. It's all in the execution, has one written a well-made, well-thought book?

The rise of hip-hop, which innovated in both the form and content of black music, highlights the point I'm making. One only has to contrast Eminem with DJ Shadow. Both are white artists who have had massive influence through the medium of hip-hop. Shadow, of course, isn't the pop star that Eminem is, but make no mistake, he is every bit as influential. Shadow's musical persona is in his sound qua sound. He took the sounds of hip-hop, its architecture—breakbeats—and pushed

---

* Mackey, Nathaniel. "Other: From Now to Verb." *Representations* 39 (Summer 1992): 51–70

** Styron, William. *The Confessions of Nat Turner*. 1967. New York: Vintage International, 1993.

them into sonic space they hadn't been before. No denotation, all connotation. Eminem on the other hand...well, I'll leave it Carl Hancock Rux to break that down:

https://www.randomhouse.com/boldtype/0303/tate/essay.html

• • •

Re: [bookclubx] podcast

Tuesday, January 18, 2011 7:31 PM
From: "egie ighile" <XXXXXX@XXXXX>
To: xbookclubx@XXXXXXXX

I can't disagree with you, Quincy, not having read the book.

I do wonder, though, about the idea of what "black people need", not necessarily with respect to this book but with respect to literature or even art in general. I know what I, personally, as a reader and as a reader who reads with the intention of writing want (need and want in this case tending to be, it would seem, the same thing, thanks to the pleasure principle).

The Confessions of Nat Turner is not a book I intend to read anytime soon because there are other renderings of consciousness that are of greater interest to me. Narratives of slavery, narratives of the "oppressed" are not of central concern to me, especially when they become taken-for-granted categories of identity. (Of course, knowledge of history and of how the present relates to it is essential. And there are works by black authors that have tilled this soil, as it relates to the traumas of black history, that I respect. I am well aware that my present existential luxuries have been bequeathed to me by ancestors.) It is foolish to talk about a book I haven't read, but even if Styron's book was written for a white audience, written to enable it rationalize a societal order, the true face of which it is by events forced to confront, even if the book were that, there is something to be said about looking into the white psyche (so far as any "race" has a monolithic psyche) through the contents of such a book, even for a black reader. If I were to read the book, that perhaps is why I would read it.

But, as I said, my central concerns lie elsewhere. I intend to stand on what has been bequeathed to me, the central legacy of which, for me, is the agency to define myself. Hence, I intend to be true to that agency irrespective of what anyone may think "black people need" or what any other people need for that matter. This is not to say that literature and narratives shouldn't be engaged with the terrain of the world or should abdicate values which connect the self to others. It is simply to say come at it slant, with imagination, and reconfigure the terrain, because the terrain of the world is the space of a mind.

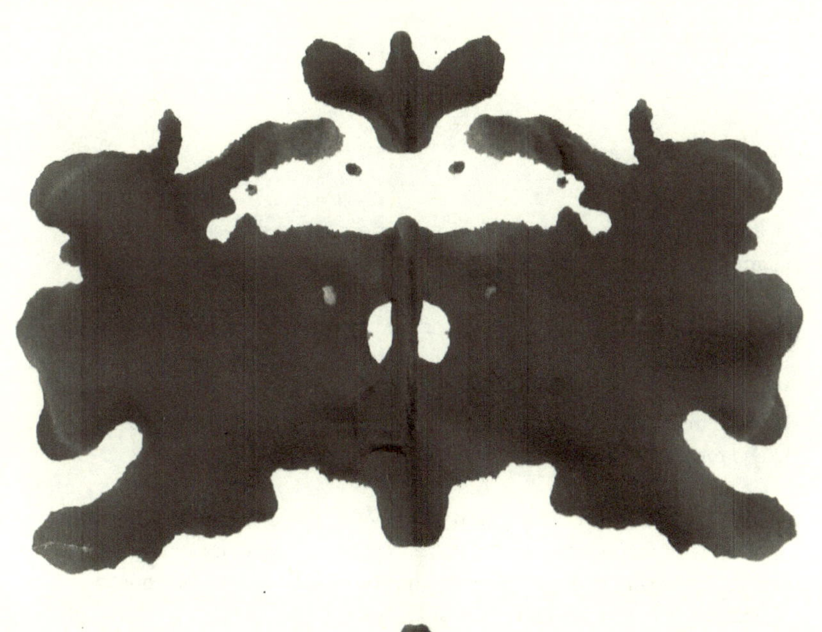

DOING WHAT IS NECESSARY AND NEEDS TO BE DONE: A ROUNDTABLE

January 27, 2011

Project Row Houses emerged in 1992 from a series of conversations among Bert Long, Jesse Lott, Rick Lowe, Bert Samples, George Smith, James Bettison and Floyd Newsum—collectively, "The Magnificent Seven"—who sought ways to support and preserve the historic community of Third Ward. The artists' concerns were remarkably resonant with the ideas explored by Book Club in 2011: how can we use our collective strengths to support our communities, create new artist opportunities, and forge new models for living creatively, gracefully, politically?

In January 2011, the six living members of The Magnificent Seven sat down with members of Book Club for an intergenerational conversation. The result is an oral history that powerfully recalls the context within which Project Row Houses was formed.

THEY LET ME OUT OF MY CAGE FOR A FEW MINUTES.

Rick Lowe: I'm Rick, Rick Lowe and I live here down the street, but not in this building.

Steffani Jemison: I'm Steffani Jemison. I live closer to this building than anybody; I'm in the Ze-Row House.

Jesse Lott: I live far away from here, I live in 5th Ward, but I got my visa extended for one day so I could come over here.

(*Laughs*)

George Smith: I'm George Smith, I am a ... I don't know, I am here, I am one of the originals

Kaneem Smith: Kaneem Smith, daughter of George Smith, I'm an art teacher, artist down the street.

Egie Ighile: I am Egie Ighile. I'm a writer.

Bert Long: I'm the ugly one so you must be the pretty one.

(**Bert Samples:** That is what they've always said: little Bert.

Rick Lowe: I've taken it over from you from time to time. [They say,] you must be ... you're Bert Long aren't you?

Bert Long: Worse than that, I met this lady a long time ago at a show down at the beach in Galveston. She says—"I know you! I know you! You are James Surls aren't you?!"

(*Laughs*)

Floyd Newsum: In Memphis they call me Floyd.

(*Don't you mess with nobody from Memphis. Floyd is always about to beat somebody up.*)

Bert Long: I'm Bert Long, I am from 5th Ward too. They let me out of my cage for a few minutes. I noticed nobody told their age. I'ma tell you, I'm 87.

(*Cheers*)

Bert Long: I think Jesse is 6–7–8–10 years older than I am

(*Laughs*)

Jesse Lott: I didn't get my birth certificate until I was 13—

(*Laughs*)

Jesse Lott: —so you have to break it down in two segments: early years and late years.

Rick Lowe: Ok; now we got that out of the way. Lemme just say, this is something we have been talking about doing for a long time: getting together again, because we used to do this a lot.

Jesse Lott: Amen Brother.

Rick Lowe: And then Steffani, who is our Core resident artist, started a book club of young artists that are all meeting and discussing issues. And one day I came in to one of these meetings and it kind of reminded me a little bit of what we were doing 20 years ago. And I was telling Steffani about it and she said maybe it should recorded. That's what made us interested to put this together and make this happen. Here we are.

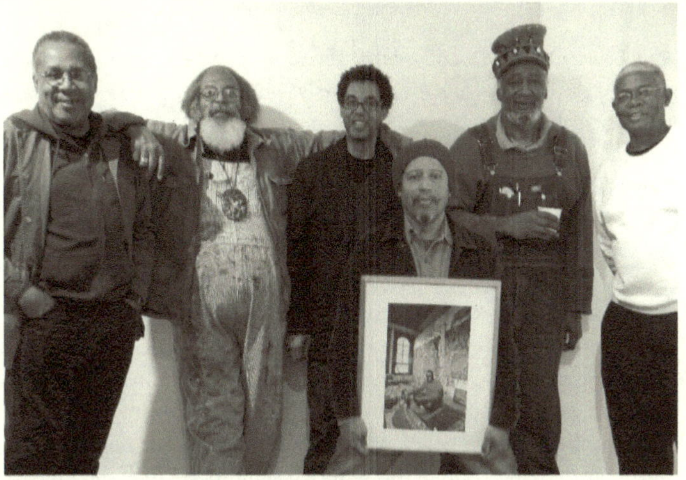

PROJECT ROW HOUSES CAME ABOUT FROM A MEETING JUST LIKE THIS.

Bert Long: Well, Row Houses, which is where we are, came about from a meeting just like this. We were sitting up in my place in the country, and I started talking about my mother living in 5th Ward. And we were just kicking ideas around. I mentioned the row houses in front of my mother's house, and I was talking about how the rent collectors would come and pick up the rent everyday. And then I [received] the Rome Prize, and next thing I heard, Rick had put all this together with Jesse and the rest of the guys. And it came from an idea, you know. We were originally thinking of turning it upside down.

Rick Lowe: I remember we were thinking of putting it next to the Bayou, it had to be next to the Bayou.

Jesse Lott: You wanna know what I remember? On our way down there I stopped at a liquor store there to get a bottle of brandy—that is what they wanted.

(*All talking over each other*)

Floyd Newsum: I didn't get one; I don't remember getting a bottle, unless it was a beer.

Rick Lowe: Ooo lord, ooo lord that was scary. I had never gone on a dirt road in the country—but even before we got there when we stopped at that place along the way—

Floyd Newsum: Klan country.

(*Everyone agrees*)

Rick Lowe: Serious Klan country!

Bert Long: Well you should know that the reason why I'm back in Houston now, is because when I was living in Spain my wife and I came back for a big show I had, and we drove to our house. It was burnt down to the ground, two walls left standing—"fuck you niggers" and swastika signs on all the walls. The bad thing about that is that I never got a notice from the police. Everybody knew who I was, but they never notified me. It was scary. I was [living] up there 14 years and it's still scary up there. You know James Surls, his wife basically told him that she was not, that they had to leave East Texas, because she was not going to bring up her girls up there. That is why he is in Colorado now. Mm hmm... Well now we came to a safe place like "Bloody 5th Ward" ... [*laughs*]...

Rick Lowe: You are at least familiar with it.

Bert Long: Well I was born there, and Jesse's been there. Jesse, were you born there?

Jesse Lott: I came right before times began. I wasn't there when they discovered black pepper, but I was there when they named it.

Bert Long: It was called "Bloody 5th" where I came from, because every night somebody died, and it is still that way to some degree.

FIFTH WARD AND THE DE LUXE SHOW

Rick Lowe: Now, were you around when The De Luxe Show* happened though?

Bert Long: I used to go [to The De Luxe movie theater] and look at Hop-a-Long Cassidy. You are talking about The De Luxe show with Mrs. de Menil and all the guys. I wasn't a part of it; I wasn't in the art world at the time. I was a chef.

Jesse Lott: They brought a lot of artists in from New York.

Rick Lowe: Oh, so you weren't around for that—(*to Bert Long*)—But *you* were—(*to Jesse Lott*)

Jesse Lott: Yeah I was there. Yeah I helped set it up, but this is the funny part. You want me to tell it?

Bert Long: You gotta tell it.

Jesse Lott: Carroll Simms was one of the brothers that was setting this thing up. And Harry Vital. Mr. V-tall, remember Mr. V-tall. His name was Harry Vital, but he got to be a professor at Texas Southern and he changed his name to Harry VEE-tall (*exaggerated pronunciation*).

Everyone: (*Laughs*) Yeah! V-Tall!

Jesse Lott: So they were selecting artists, and at first they were selecting local artists, but as the notoriety about the upcoming show got to be greater and greater, it started to change and [they started] putting in big timers, New York artists, really.

Rick Lowe: Were [Dr. John] Biggers and Simms even in it, in the show?

---

* The De Luxe Show was an historic art exhibition organized by the Menil Foundation. One of the first racially integrated exhibitions of contemporary art in the United States, the show was held in the De Luxe movie theater in the heart of Houston's Fifth Ward.

Jesse Lott: No, they were running it.

Rick Lowe: Oh they were running it.

Jesse Lott: They were the ones that did the set up and the presentation, and as a matter of fact I was the last local artist to get excluded!

(*Laughs*)

Jesse Lott: You know, and the exhibition was supposed to be about black art in 5th Ward, and where my studio is right now is only about 6 blocks away from it, right down the street from it.

Bert Long: You were right up the street from The Roxy.

Jesse Lott: Yeah.

Bert Long: We were allowed to go to the Roxy.

Jesse Lott: (*Laughs*)

Bert Long: The Roxy was where, you know...

Jesse Lott: It was rough

Bert Long: It was rough all the girls had short skirts.

Jesse Lott: It was rough. It was the roughest part of 5th Ward. They called it Pearl Harbor, you've heard of that? Remember Ron? Ron Wilson, he was our representative.

Bert Long: Yes, I remember Ron.

Jesse Lott: One of our state representatives, he did his campaign speech directly across the street from where my studio is. I'll never forget it—he said, "I am coming to you from the worst part of the worst neighborhood in the United States of America."

Bert Long: Well do you realize that there, where they are doing a lot of building, has the lowest per capita income in any city, place in Texas? Right now.

Jesse Lott: I know. That's why there is no people there no more.

(*Laughs*)

Bert Samples: They are still knocking houses. Well there is a reason for that. People that lived in little framed houses, they are used to paying less than $100 a month.

Bert Long: Right.

Bert Samples: When you put a townhouse up there, you have to go up to $900... you know, $1,500.

Everyone: Mmm-hmm.

THIS GUY LOOKS LIKE AN ARTIST

Bert Long: You are talking about those New York artists; we got a New York artist here [*pointing to George Smith*].

(*Laughs*)

Rick Lowe: He was brought in to civilize you.

(*Laughs*)

Bert Long: He came here as a New York artist but he been napped a lot.

(*Laughs*)

Rick Lowe: So that is right, George so you came here straight to teach at Rice, or...?

George Smith: Yeah. They wouldn't say it, but they recruited me. The reason why I said OK is because Jim Harithas was down here, and I kinda talked with him a little bit. He said yeah it's cool.

Rick Lowe: Did you know him from before?

George Smith: Yeah, he gave me my first one-man show in New York.

Rick Lowe: Oh, Okay.

George Smith: He gave me a show at the Everson [Museum in Syracuse], and from there he went to another museum and gave me a show there, so things were happening from Jim and became good friends. He was a professor at Hunter College when I met him, and what was good about Jim is that Jim was a trying to integrate, well it was integrated anyway, but he was trying to put blacks in his class.

Bert Samples: Tell us the story about the class and about how you were perceived.

George Smith: How I was perceived? What do you mean by that?

(Jumbled talking, laughing)

Jesse Lott: No he's talking about the canvas rip up.

George Smith: I did a piece where I ripped a canvas up, a big roll of canvas, and it was really a music piece like, *(laughs)* because I rolled the paper on jazz, and then I took a hula-hoop, or not a hula-hoop, a fire hose, or what do you call that—the pipe that they use to clean the water. The corrugated pipe, what do you call it? Used in swimming pools. You can roll it up and make sound with it, but I had a big one and it made a sound. We were on the roof at Hunter College; we were like 15 floors up. Some of the administration came out to see what was going on.

Bert Long: So when they saw you ripping up that, they said, "Uh-oh, maybe we made a mistake."

(Laughs)

George Smith: No, but you know the funny thing about that is that a lot of people in the class, in particular white artists cause most of them were, there were three black artists, they would know a lot about conceptual stuff, so it wasn't anything different. It's just that when I did it, I was perceived as angry, but I was just doing conceptual stuff.

Bert Long: It is better that way. I always tell this story about John Alexander. We would be at the parties and stuff and John be talking to all the women and kissing on them and all those things, everything. So one day, I kissed Kathy Whitmire, now we all know that he was the cowboy with white gloves and everything else, but when I did it, I wasn't invited to any more parties.

(*Laughs*)

Bert Long: For a long time, they actually, they black balled me. Kathy Whitmire was the mayor; she was the first woman mayor here. I mean, well may be it's the way we dress or something. But remember when we showed up at the CAMH [Contemporary Art Museum Houston] for that show? I was kinda cleaned up at that time, I may have had my briefcase on me. Jesse was like he is right there [*wearing denim overalls*] they met me, and looked at Jesse...

(*Laughs*)

Rick Lowe: This guys looks like an artist, this guy...

(*Laughs*)

Jesse Lott: Let me tell you what happened... I was working across the street, over where Harris Gallery is now.

Rick Lowe: Oh, Anne's place.

Jesse Lott: They called us the rats. Everybody that worked there was artists, and we worked as a team to do things, mainly put on exhibitions and then we would do our work. The people across the street were more in the upper level of stuff; they were still doing a lot on New York stuff.

YOU DIDN'T WAIT TO BE ASKED?

Rick Lowe: Then Linda Cathcart.*

(Oh boy...)

Rick Lowe: And then the Cathcart era.

(Everyone remembers Linda Cathcart)

George Smith: She was in classes with me in New York. She wouldn't talk to me here though.

Rick Lowe: Yeah that was around the time I was thinking about Houston. When I was in school and I looked in magazines, she popped up a lot, in association with Houston.

Jesse Lott: Yeah, she kinda liked to establish New York in Houston.

Rick Lowe: Yeah it was like Schnabel, well he was kind of from here, but [David] Salle and [Richard] Longo...

Jesse Lott: When was all that work?

Rick Lowe: 1980, '81, something like that.

Floyd Newsum: They used to have these art galleries at Rice in Sewall Hall in the back of this auditorium, and she had invited the director that founded the New Museum in New York, Marcia Tucker. And Marcia is going to be showing what is new, the upcoming artists that she has been looking at in the New York area. So the rumors went that there was a lot of dealers and the art community there, and then Linda Cathcart was invited to show who she's been looking at, and she was going to show New York artists as well, so no one in Houston [was represented]. The only person that she showed, the only African American artist, was Robert Colescott. She showed the painting that he

* As Director of the Contemporary Arts Museum Houston during the 1980s, Cathcart oversaw several important exhibitions, including the influential 1984 exhibition *The Heroic Figure*, which included work by Robert Longo, Julian Schnabel, David Salle, and other well-known artists.

did [reworking "Potato Eaters by] Vincent van Gogh, called "Eat dem Taters." Me and George just looked at each other, and I just remember that look that I had, and I remember the look that he had, like, "We are going to be the first ones out of here."

(*Laughs*)

Rick Lowe: You didn't wait to be asked?

Floyd Newsum: We didn't wait. It was interesting what Jesse talked about cause my perception of The De Luxe Show [was different]: I didn't realize that Dr. Biggers and Carroll Simms were involved in the conceptualizing of it. All I remember was an artist, I think his name was Peter, but he was the son of Miles Davis.

George Smith: Peter Bradley.

(*Everyone agrees*)

Floyd Newsum: They brought him in to organize and curate the show.

Rick Lowe: That is probably how, like a lot of things happen, they start out locally and then it's like, now we have to bring in somebody in from the big city to help them out.

THE TIME WHEN WE FIRST GOT TOGETHER

Floyd Newsum: That was so emblematic of a lot of stuff that had been going on because that was in the 70's and from the time that we started coming together, we would have to go to each other. Like the first thing I remember is—

Bert Long: How did we get together?

Floyd Newsum: I remember we got a show together.

Rick Lowe: Midtown.

Floyd Newsum: Midtown.

Rick Lowe: Yeah, that was in '86. The building where the Community Artists' Collective [currently] is, there was another building next to it with studios. At that time, there was DiverseWorks, Lawndale [Art Center], Midtown, the Firehouse, and the Art League.

Floyd Newsum: Yeah but it was one of those things where we didn't wait on anybody. We were probably selected invisibly because it was a group show or something like that. There was time for us to put a show together on our own resources, and there was a small gallery upstairs. I think you curated that show...

Rick Lowe: Who did put that together? I just remember the gallery floor was very swollen.

Floyd Newsum: And I remember that piece that Jesse did of that dog made of broken pieces of furniture. It sat in two positions: upright, and then you could rock it back, and as soon as you rocked it back it sounded like the dog was growling. The reason why I bring this up is because we were all at that opening and it was more than just us, Fletcher was in that show as well. Fletcher Mackey.

Rick Lowe: Was it put together by the Midtown folks though? Ren Houser, those folks weren't there?

Floyd Newsum: No no, it was us.

Rick Lowe: Jesse, do you remember who put that show together at Midtown, the one that we were all in, the one that had the small gallery upstairs? Bert is calling that out as the first time that we all showed together.

Floyd Newsum: Y'all had been established longer than I had.

Bert Long: That was all part of Artists in Action. We started sending out cards for Artists in Action. We would send our business cards out, the people, and anyone that wanted to be part of this group could send a business card with a picture, or a picture with their phone number. And then it was basically I am a member of Artists in Action, when am I gonna have a show? You call five people, and those five had obligation to show five, and so here is an artist that had never had a show that had 500 people at their opening. We did that forever.

Jesse Lott: It was the crowd concept.

Bert Long: The crowd concept.

Jesse Lott: It is really a pyramid scheme, a pyramid scheme without having to really risk any money. (*Laughs*) All you risk is your presence. You see what I am saying, if you have presence, you got people there, you can make money, but you need to have a crowd in art to get the notoriety. So what we had was a scheme to get a crowd. It was a bait thing, where you would bait them by the previous exhibition, which you tell them what they missed, but it was a non-existent exhibition, missed. And you can be at the next one if you registered, and brought people.

(*Talking and laughing over each other: Oh yeah! Artists in Action*)

Bert Long: And the whole thing was really involved in where you [Floyd] have been a professor forever now at the University of Houston Downtown.

(*Laughs*)

Floyd Newsum: And then Little Bert is doing a piece there right now.

Bert Long: You and I did a show there, and I did a big ice piece inside. In fact you guys published one of the first posters did them, and I still have that poster. It's in my archive now, right there. A lot happened between Fifth Ward and Third Ward. For people that don't know: Fifth was Bloody Fifth and then Third Ward was Sadity Town. I was working the Houston clubs, and I had my silk suits with a cane and alligator shoes. And so, I would come out here to Eldorado and Club Sadity. You understand? That's where all the jazz was. That is why I knew about the Eldorado. During those times I could get in anywhere even though, I was only 16–17. I have always been this size, and I shopped.

(*Laughs*)

Bert Long: You are laughing! But one time I went to The De Luxe Show in The De Luxe Theater, and we say, "But he's only 12." He says, "No no no no. He gotta pay adult fare."

Rick Lowe: So Bert took us to the time when we first got together.

NO ONE BACKED DOWN

Floyd Newsum: Like we said we didn't know each other that well. I known Bert the longest, and I've known Jesse for a long time. When we got together it was an interesting kind of spark. Because the thing I remember was that just the way we played dominos, I always thought it was very in your face. No one backed down and if you backed down you weren't gonna hang with that group. I just remember that time after we had that show in Midtown, we came down and sat down on the corner and for some reason—was it Rodney Ellis?—it was some congressman that drove by. This when I recognized the genius of Jesse, cause Jesse took opportunities to challenge and take it to the next step. We were talking about, "How can we convince the people on the other side of the track to give young artists opportunities?" And Jesse would sau, "You don't need to convince anybody."

Bert Long: Listen. I want to jump in the bandwagon, because I owe a lot to that man right there.

Jesse Lott: You're my man.

(*Laughs*)

Bert Long: I first came down here, and I was craving a little excitement in the art world. I went over to Jesse, and every time I do lectures I tell people about this. One of the most important things I've ever heard, especially being an artist of color, we will all together will have to deal with the system being an artist of color, and Jesse said, "You are out here, you are doing it, you are making the waves. You are going to have to learn a couple of things. You gotta learn the language of art and be able to talk." Then he said, "You shouldn't be so worried about trying to fit into their system, you should create your own system, and they'll come to your system." That's it. I started writing in the newspapers. I wrote an article about the Museum of Fine Arts, and an article called "A Fish Pinched from his Head First." And man, let me tell you...

(*Laughs*)

Bert Long: From New York to here... Linda Carthart calls James Surls and said—"Is that?" He says—"Well you know art, I mean." And she said—"Wait. It says on here that you are the international editor for this paper."

(Someone): What is the paper again?

Bert Long: *Art Scene*, it's all in microfiche. I made sure that was put in on the record for the history down at the library. It's stamped. You know how that came about. You want to control something on press. Those are the things that Jesse and Artists in Action taught all of us. We haven't talked about you. My brother here Bert Samples has been there in the thick of an elitist crowd forever. He's a top curator at the Museum of Fine Arts.

Bert Samples: Top curator?

(*Laughs*)

Bert Long: Well you were one of the only ones.

Bert Samples: I'm just a brother behind the scenes.

Rick Lowe: You were one of the first in the Core program, right?

Bert Samples: Yes. Second one.

Rick Lowe: Second group...

Bert Long: How many years has it been?

Bert Samples: Like 29. [*Laughs*]

Rick Lowe: Okay. So, going back to that show, that was the first time.

Bert Samples: That was the first show, before there were Jesse and Bert or Jesse and Floyd for a show. But as for what I recollect, the initiative, the idea came from us. It wasn't that we were selected by somebody else to be in the show. And I credited Floyd because he was the artist in residence at that gallery space. Maybe it was Fletcher.

Jesse Lott: It might have been Fletcher.

(*Everyone agrees.*)

Bert Samples: Yeah, Fletcher.

Bert Long: Fletcher is at the Maryland Institute now, isn't he?

Bert Samples: Yeah, yeah. That makes sense.

Jesse Lott: That was well before Snug Harbor.*

Rick Lowe: That was the fourth show, and see now that is another key point. See I remember Snug Harbor was in '92, but before that I started to get really close to Bert Samples through the Union of Independent Artists. But I really started connecting with Bert when we started organizing The Union of Independent Artists (UIA).

Bert Samples: I remember you calling and saying, "I want to show you something," one morning. You pull up right by the row houses, and they were all boarded up at that point. Then that's when I know we started having more regular meetings, and that is the transition from the UIA to Row Houses. We started meeting at Michelle Barnes' place, at the [Community Artists'] Collective. We were using some of the resources of the Collective and the UIA because the UIA had started a newsletter. We did several events. We did a show: we protested in front of this corporation's building on San Felipe...

Rick Lowe: Do you remember the one that had a running tree?

Bert Samples: The one that had the puppets and the running tree.

---

* "1992 The Americas?" was an exhibition of public art at Snug Harbor in Staten Island, New York, featuring work by Jesse Lott and Rick Lowe.

Rick Lowe: That was one of the best protests I've ever seen. I remember we were protesting the cutting down of the red woods, and so we made this big papier-mâché tree with somebody in it. And so the tree would go to the lawn and when the police come, the tree would run back. It was beautiful man! Every time the police would come the tree came running back. That was a great scene.

(*Everyone agrees.*)

Bert Long: The last meeting I remember, was when we wanted to do the suitcase project.

Jesse Lott: Oh yeah. That is a good one.

Bert Long: Each one of us would do a print that would fit into a suitcase, and it would go somewhere. You could sell prints out of there. We should still do that show because we haven't done anything collective lately.

DOING WHAT WAS NECESSARY AND NEEDED TO BE DONE

Rick Lowe: I knew Bert [Long], kinda from Commerce Street because we were around there with The Union of Independent Artists. I think I knew you guys on periphery. I didn't really *know* you, but there was a sense at a certain point, that I had, that I was the last one of us to come to town. I came in, and I jumped right in with the Commerce Street art scene, and you know, it took me about a year to start. But there was this kind of natural yearning, to say, "I'm here, there are all these white artists, this [is] a community of people," but there was something that was missing. That is when I started thinking more about Biggers and that whole African American art side. I had started out in a place where that was not even on the radar at all.

Bert Long: I am sitting here now, and I am saying to myself, "I'm really proud of the fact that we did it. Well, we are still doing it. But we were never attacking the white artists. We didn't even talk about them. It was just about us doing what was necessary and needed to be done."

Rick Lowe: Yeah.

Bert Long: There was always a focus of, "Okay, what can we do next?" And it wasn't about, "Okay, we are gonna make some money." It was about, "Okay, what can we do to try to enhance the situation. That's our obligation as artists." That came from [Dr. Biggers] too. Every time I write something, [I am stating that] I have an obligation as an artist, and that came from him too.

Rick Lowe: Yeah. I really started to realize that I needed that connection when we were working with UIA. We started to do things connected with issues that were relevant to black people. And then all of a sudden, the UIA started saying—and all those people started saying—"Wait a minute, we don't want to go to that S.H.A.P.E. community center and do anything. That doesn't have anything to to do with us. I mean, the group started doing all these protests. I mean, we did the redwoods one, we did one down at the Gloria Kelly were there was a medical waste facility, the freedom of expression, the Persian Gulf War. Everybody was enthusiastic. Everybody was down with that. They were all over it. Then when we said, there is this police brutality thing that is happening, you know? We should show our voice, and all of a sudden it was like: [*silence*].

(*Laughs*)

Bert Samples: I remember talking to the group and saying, "We are in a poisonous community. Artists in Houston have no voice, and we instead of sitting back like years and years expecting for this dealer, or that collector to pull us out, we said, "Well, we'll just do it on our own. We don't need no gallery. We'll show in our warehouse spaces, in our studios, we can get the word out." So we are empowering the whole artist community. But then it's like you said, when we wanted to focus on African American communities, like Third Ward, that is when [we realized] what it was. We had this clique over here, this clique over there, and it wasn't no unity. Because it sounded like an oxymoron: a union of independent artists. You know? It just didn't fit, but it worked for a short time, and people put a lot of time in it.

Rick Lowe: It was 500 members at one point. It was huge.

Bert Samples: And so I remember when I got my degree, my sister looked at it and she just laughed. She said, "What the hell are you gonna do with this?"

Bert Samples: [*Laughing*] You might as well work at the post office. So that kind of dark future that was always brewing there. Then, when I started connecting with you guys there was no kind of defeatism in the language in the presentation. We weren't only representing ourselves; we were representing younger people that were coming, that hadn't been there yet. When they arrive they have something to move towards, there is already a trail that has been established. That was the best thing about the Row Houses. Everyone can find a warehouse and sit in their space, but it is always in a part of town where there is no activity, except for the nine to five hours. All the kids from the suburbs congregate there all weekend, and hang out, but these were the places where we lived and worked, and they would just be there for a few hours and then move on. They had no interaction with anybody or anything. Now it may have been industrial, but there were people living on the next block. This is the first time I can see were you have an active organization that is engaged with the community around them.

HOW DID YOU GET THAT JOB?

Floyd Newsum: Bert, how did you get that job?

(*Laughs*)

Rick Lowe: (mocking) How did you get that job?

(*Laughs*)

Bert Samples: I don't know if I want to go down that road, but...

(*Laughs*)

Rick Lowe: He don't wanna give away the secret.

(*Laughs*)

Floyd Newsum: I'll tell you how I got mine, kinda like George. When I had come down here in '76, I had already gone and accepted [a teaching position at] Prairie View A&M and I was hired, but I had this one question.

I asked President Thompson, I said, "President Thompson, now I have been trained at all these different schools, and all these schools taught me a lot of things I want to teach African Americans." He said, "What do you mean?" I said, "Well look, I know that at most African American schools they never teach figure drawing." He said, "What is figure drawing?" I said, "Well it's drawing the nude." He says, "Huh?" (*Laughs*) He said, "Well if the boys' women come around here, they'll get upset." So I went to Philly and I call my dad. I say, "Dad, I got a job down in Texas in this place called Prairie View, and I don't know what it is. It's some country, I didn't even see any big buildings." (*Laughs*) "I am scared to go down there because the guy will not let me teach what I would like to teach the brothers and sisters." He said, "Son you know you gotta wife and a baby coming, and so you might want to reconsider. You might want to take that job." And I said to myself, "If I go down there, I am gonna feel really upset, and I won't be able to function." So I declined.

So for a whole year I worked as a postman, taught part-time, and worked at Sears. I sent my resume to [University of Houston], and I got a letter saying they had transferred my resume from the central campus to downtown campus. So, I get an interview. I got over there. I got off the airplane, and the chairperson met me. We were driving, he said—"Look now don't be nervous." Then I said, "Mmm-hmm." I ain't nervous, I have been practicing for all these years, visiting all over the country. I said, "No problem." So I said to myself, I got to the interview, and I actually carried the interview, cause there weren't any art people there, so I had to make conversation about what I needed to do and what I wanted to do. So actually I already knew I had the job. Then when I got there I thought I was the second of color. And so it was a blessing, cause they needed some of us, I guess, being the second. But you know my history is that I had to fight. But that is fine with me cause I be struggling.

Bert Long: Well, look at Dr. Biggers. How did we get to Texas Southern? It's always about somebody helping you. I had a great show at the

Museum of Fine Arts and everything, but I don't mind saying that there are a lot of elements to that. Sure, my work had to measure up and everything, but it also happened because they thought I was dying. You understand? Those things enter into it. If it hadn't been for James Surls, if I hadn't met this man here [*pointing to Jesse*], a lot of things would be different—my whole philosophy came from you [*Jesse*] and Salvador Dali.

Jesse: Two crazy people. [*Laughs*]

Bert Long: The only [art] class that I had in 5th Ward was with Mrs. Ladner at Phyllis Wheatley High School.

Jesse Lott: Man, don't forget Ms. Manor.

Bert Long: I didn't have really no art classes with her.

Jesse Lott: You didn't? Oh she was good.

Bert Long: I was told that there was only one other African American artist or black artist at that time. He was at the school, and he was really a great draughtsman. So they told him that he could be an artist at some illustration firm and stuff like that. And basically they told me that there was no possibility for me to be an artist. No possibility. They still tell me this. (*Laughs*) No. I am saying because, right now, of all those people that went to Texas Southern and African American universities, real honest, wanting to be artists, how many actually go on to really live it? All of us are living it. Rick does his art in different ways, he is not making objects, but he is still doing his art. He moved over into the "Nude Descending the Stairs," that kind of a thing, you understand, concepts and stuff like that. (*Laughs*) But we are still making our art. We are still doing it.

TOWARD A DEFINITION OF "BLACK ART"

Rick Lowe: Yeah, but one thing we haven't brought up in this, was James Bettison, the Ball of Energy.

Bert Long: We are missing him.

Rick Lowe: He was really a whirlwind of energy that was kind of moving and hitting everybody that came his way.

Bert Long: I got two pieces of his hanging in my house.

Jesse Lott: He's the individual, you see? He went beyond qualifications and pigeonholes. You could not pin Big James down in a category. He was Black. He didn't do no Black art. He didn't do no White art either. He didn't do no conceptual art. Never, never, he accepted no categorization. That is what I liked about him.

Bert Long: You can say that about all of us, though. Jesse: we are all African American artists, but we are not known for making Black art. John Ross, he is one of the greatest modernists ever. You understand? Okay, and Bert Samples. I like his drawings, they're as great as anything. Your abstraction. And if someone were to look through the 3000 pieces of work I have made, they could put a show about being Black together. They could put a show together of fence posts, because I take thousands of them.

Bert Samples: How do you define Black art though?

Bert Long: Well, I didn't go to school! I didn't go to school, so I am using it loosely. I am talking about Black genre.

Jesse Lott: Some reference to the Black social development, the Black sensibilities, and sometimes it is actually done by Black people.

(*Laughs*)

Bert Samples: Like you say, you defy all types of categories. And we were all defying those categorizations ourselves, because we were trying to grow out of something that didn't have no future. It didn't have no future at least in the Houston community. So we were redefining ourselves. But I really think that change was really the catalyst for that because you have to accept James in his own terms. You know?

Rick Lowe: And he always had that entry, he wanted to do something. "Lets do something." You know? That was his thing. "Lets do something, let's do it, let's do it." At that time when we were all coming together, I know that for myself being new in town trying to find my way and find connections. George, you were kind of over at Rice, in that different world. It was obvious that there weren't a lot of black artists in this town. So when we were starting to come together, you had people that you had trained and taught.

FL: Yeah, but they were not getting opportunities.

Rick Lowe: Now, when I come to the Book Club here I can see a whole other generation. And then there is like another pocket of African American artists that kind of Tierney Malone and those guys that do their thing. It's a completely different dynamic now than it was then.

Jesse Lott: I can tell you that the difference is that right now it is wide open, back then it was closed shut.

Floyd Newsum: It sure was.

Jesse Lott: They only let one or two through the door.

Bert Samples: That was the moment that the Museum desegregated their policies. It was that they had an annual competition rejoining who won first place, first prize that he was not able to attend his opening because it was like on Friday and—

Jesse Lott: We could only go on Thursday.

Bert Samples: or Sunday.

Jesse Lott: (*laughing*) Yeah!

Bert Samples: I have a picture of this teacher taking their students through the south gate and going up the stairs looking at one of the sculptures. That happened to him at the MFAH it happened also in Dallas but in a worse way, because when he won first prize and he came to the museum to receive his check, the didn't even let him into the building. They just opened the door and just gave him the check.

(*Laughs*)

Bert Samples: So here we have someone who is this great icon because now he is international but at the time, those policies were so entrenched that it sharpened the vision of the students at that time. "How can I even compare myself to Dr. Biggers, what would it take?" And the characters that they would beat into you every day you were there was perseverance. I mean, hammering you down. It is what they call running through the fire.

Bert Long: I think it is one of the more important traits, and that is why I brought it up twice now, and he just brought it up. I think it is almost a miracle that we are still here.

Bert Samples: Schools had the same problem in Maryland. I mean that is something that happened to a lot of Black artists across the country.

TO BE AN ARTIST PRACTICING IN HOUSTON

Rick Lowe: Let me ask you this. I want to tie into your thing about the fact that Biggers, you know, back then it was a certain way, and now he is known. Whatever, but still there is a sense in my mind that the stature of John Biggers, the level of his work and his accomplishments is still not acknowledged at a level that it should be. I'm gonna bring this into a broader conversation about what happens, cause I think that Biggers is a little regionalized, basically. You know? And we are all sitting here as artists that, and usually regionalized means that you are not in New York, right? Cause New York is a region too, but they don't consider themselves a region. So we are all chose to live here, to make this our home, but all to our own satisfaction do things in different places to fill what we desire. Basically, I guess that is to match whatever our ambition is with our work and how we see it, what role we see it playing. That is a question about what it means to be an artist practicing in Houston, not so much just among ourselves among the generations here, but relative to the greater context.

Bert Long: I'm gonna say that it is not only being African American and working in Houston, it is being still as an African American artist period on the national and international scene. And, listen to hundreds and hundreds of lectures showing stuff and out in the public and different places. I had one of my biggest collectors say,

"Bert, why are you complaining? You've made money. And that is nice, but I don't see 20 million dollar commissions like Richard Serra, you understand? Mel makes a lot of money, but we haven't reached that point. We are not there.

Rick Lowe: Even when you start looking at the younger generation of people, when you start looking at people like Julie Mehretu and Mark Bradford, the young hot artists that are selling work for big dollars. And I caught myself thinking this the other day, cause I was with Mark the other day. We were at his gallery, and there were pieces that were on the waiting list, and they were two hundred, three hundred thousand, whatever. But then there are people on the other side [making more money], and you think *what* other people, you know? I mean, [two hundred thousand] is a lot of money, but it is still not at all what, I mean, it is not comparable.

Bert Long: I want to say this. Houston has been great to me. Houston and a lot of great things have happened to me, but I spent my whole lifetime trying to get the hell out of here. (*Laughs*) It is true! And it is not arrogance or anything. My goal is to try to realize my potential fully. Truthfully, I was telling Floyd today, I wouldn't be back in Houston. I had already made up my mind to stay in Europe and to deal with New York and not to come back. I came back because my wife died and then I got involved. And now it is out of the question to go. But that is the reality of living in Houston. I mean, even if you are so called "successful"... But Houston has been good to me. Houston is still a place where you can make things happen.

Right now the gallery scene here and everything is totally flat. There is only one or two places that are really showing on the international scene. I mean if anybody is showing. Nathaniel, he is talking about a bigger picture. We have talked about it too before. You persevere and really you hammer and you hammer and you hammer. Like Jewish groups: don't let them forget. That is why I am glad to be here with you, dear [*to Steffani*]. Don't let them forget, this still happened. We are here now, it is on the record. It is important. We have an obligation and a role to play, to be a mirror of what has happened. It will pay off and they will have a map. You understand?

I didn't have a map. I read every book I could. That is where it came from.

George Smith: I started at North Carolina A&T And I left there because there was a woman there, a practician there, and she said, "If you really want to be an artist, you are too good to be here." She said, "You need to go to New York."

(*Laughs*)

George Smith: No, seriously. And then she bought me a book, and it was a book on John Biggers. You know? But I had never known other than Dr. Leroy Holmes and other few other black people, Richard Hunt.

Bert Long: Richard Hunt was my connection.

George Smith: Yeah, mine too. I didn't know anything about black artists, so he brought me this book, and it was about John Biggers. That is why I mention it, the book, cause there is a book.

Bert Long: I have it, and I am glad you brought up Richard Hunt.

George Smith: It was inspiring to see it.

Bert Long: Richard Hunt was the first. He was the first artist I met in New York, and I took time and visited him in the studio. That was my first connection with the international art world there. It was with Richard Hunt. God, he's... I think of you when I look at his drawings. You understand? I mean you guys are great draftsmen on paper and stuff.

Bert Samples: I've visited him. I've searched him out. We went out to dinner. He took me to an opera. He is really into opera and stuff like that.

Bert Long: Absolutely. He is still ahead of his time.

Bert Samples: Yeah he is.

WHEN RICK WAS A BOY

Thelma Smith: Can I tell my Rick story?

Rick Lowe: Oh lord! I don't wanna be here.

Thelma Smith: It is just a little story. It is something; it makes me feel good when I think about it. When Rick was a boy.

Bert Long: You mean he had hair?

Thelma Smith: With the hair, yeah. I think he had a studio I think in the Heights or something like that. He would come to visit the Rothko Chapel where I was working. Do you remember those days? Oh my goodness.

Rick Lowe: Oh yes. Those were drinking days.

Thelma Smith: Well, the person working in the chapel, her name was Lucia, and I don't know if Rick knew this but he was not the perfect person. He had a lot of nerve for her being the color that he was with this hair, and coming into the chapel all the time; all loud and just like paying no attention to her. She was... Well I don't want to sound prejudice, but I guess I can. She didn't have children, she didn't like children, but she certainly didn't like certain children.

(*Laughs*)

Thelma Smith: Rick would come in there. It was just; I could see her skin crawl. She had this hair, this white hair that was real stiff. You remember her?

Rick Lowe: I remember her.

Thelma Smith: Hee hee. He would come in there with his friends talking. And I'll never forget—this is the part that I really always want to remember about Rick. Rick was then and is today the same person. I remember that at the Rothko Chapel they have a lot of discussions and things like that, but I don't remember the exact topic that this was, but they were filming and everything. And so, Rick probably won't even remember this, he went outside and he was sitting on the bench and this Caucasian man he came outside also, and he is talking and talking. In a sense, he was about to say that certain people deserve to be on a higher level than others. Needless to say, you know, Rick was not having that, so they got in a discussion, an argument. I remember Rick saying something like, "So you think that that man working at the plant is not as good as this other man." You know? And Rick was just as direct.

Rick Lowe: I kinda remember that one too.

Thelma Smith: And I was pretty impressed, I said—"Alright!"

(*Laughs*)

Thelma Smith: Because I appreciate the fact that he would confront this person like that. You know? Because he had no right, I felt, to you know.

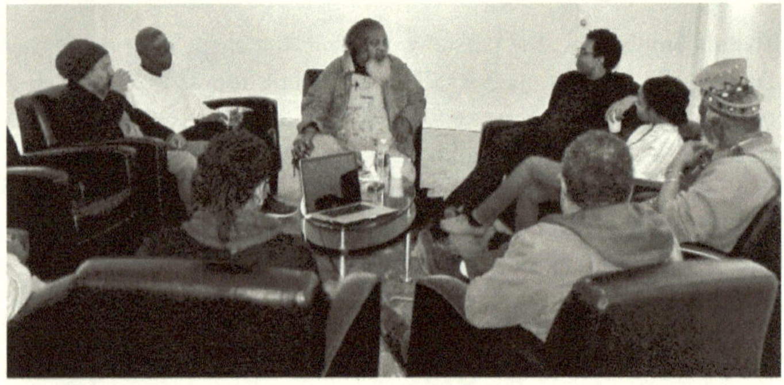

Rick Lowe: Well you know probably to my fault. I haven't figured out to say things...

Bert Long: Diplomatically

Rick Lowe: Diplomatically.

Thelma Smith: Yeah, yeah.

Rick Lowe: That lady you are talking about at the Rothko, that was one of my first connections with Dominique de Menil because one the habit that Nestor, my old running mate that I had at the time, we would come in there on Sundays kind of hung-over.

Thelma Smith: Oh God.

Rick Lowe: It was a peaceful place to recuperate. So we would go in there, and at that time they didn't have those glass doors and all that stuff. It was much more open, and people would be doing Tai Chi, whatever. And we would go in there and lay down on those benches, and that lady came, that's why I remember that she didn't like me because she came up and said, "You are not supposed to lay down on the benches." And Dominique came in there at that time and told her "Leave them alone."

Thelma Smith: Yes.

Rick Lowe: "Leave them alone. What's wrong with what they are doing?" And that is when she really hated me then.

Thelma Smith: But Mrs. de Menil has done the same thing to me. She was coming in. See I'm, I was a little bit in fear with people, and this couple was on the bench with their heads pointed towards and their feet on the end pointed like this. And Mrs. de Menil was coming, an I thought, "Oh Lord I'm gonna have to get these people up. So I went in to tell them to get up, and Mrs. de Menil got back to the door, and she saw what I was doing. She pointed her finger at me and did like this [*gestures*].

(*Laugh*)

Thelma Smith: OK

Bert Long: Mrs. de Menil, the great thing about her in art history, being a black artist in Houston, is that she would always invite me, especially when I was doing the paper, to her private dinners. I haven't been invited to one since she died.

(*Laughs*)

Bert Long: When I did my first monumental ice piece at the 12th International Sculpture Conference in San Francisco. Mrs. de Menil wrote the first check: two hundred dollars. It is somewhere in my archive. She wrote the first check. She was always there. The De Luxe Show we talk about in the beginning, that was Mrs. Dominique de Menil.

MY BRIAR PATCH

Rick Lowe: I want to say something about the out-of-town, in-town thing. It has always been interesting for me, being in this kind of group. Cause I always knew from meeting Bert. I always knew that he wanted out of here, I mean, when he was in Spain. And then I also at the same time got to know Jesse, who is somebody who really didn't want to leave Fifth Ward.

(*Laughs*)

Rick Lowe: And so it was always this kind of nice balance for me to understand that it works that way. Some people just have a need to do this, some don't, and Jesse, I kind of have a sense of why you are comfortable. Can you talk a little bit about it?

Jesse Lott: Yeah. You know anything about Uncle Remus?

Rick Lowe: A little bit.

Jesse Lott: You ever read the story about the rabbit, the fox, and the tar baby?

Bert Long: Yep.

Rick Lowe: Tell it.

Jesse Lott: Well, Fifth Ward is my briar patch. I am comfortable right there. I can run through the briars and run through the bushes. Never have to worry, you know what I'm saying? I am at home. And it is all about what it takes to give you that validation that every human being needs. Some people think of money, but how many millions of dollars do you have to have? Bill Gates is still working. Why? Everybody needs something else. As artists, what do we have to offer? You are only as powerful as your sphere of influence. If you are doing what you can where you are, that is the best you can do.

(*Everyone agrees*)

Jesse Lott: Or you can go somewhere else and do something else that you can't do.

(*Laughs*)

WE ARE NOT AN ISLAND UNTO OURSELVES.

Rick Lowe: I want to go back and say one thing. There was something I said earlier that I wanna clean up a little bit, or at least connect it, put it in context. And I am saying this to honor Jesse in his teaching way, the way that Bert has done here. I was talking about the issue with the Union of Independent Artists—being a leader in that group, starting to do things in the African American community, and not having support of the broader group. I had [previously] been developing this attitude: I am going to TSU, I am discovering my Black side, I am going to involve myself and surround myself in a place where I belong. But at that point, I was about to just move away. It was through coming together in this group—and Jesse has always had this comfort level about where he lived, where he worked, what his work was all about—that was whole thing that opened me up. That actually allowed Project Row Houses to happen. I actually sat around and talked about these ideas. When we started working over [at Project Row Houses] it was all kind of people, from all over. So that same thing that felt defeating at one point, when people wouldn't come to support something that was happening around the Black cause, later proved itself to be the opposite. That was kind of an interesting twist.

Bert Samples: I think that we all individually prior to that had made some types of investments into our future and their future. Because we are all very engaged, working around different parts of the city doing things. So we had, even at the early stage, created kind of a trust organism, stability. If those guys come together, if they are that committed to doing something, I know if they have done it in the past, maybe we need to get behind this. And it probably wasn't just a collective awareness, but I think that it came to that point at some point, but just a continuation of meeting. You know, for artists to meet as a group. That is just a unique phenomenon, particularly back then, because you are still around this old kind of paradox, "I just need to be working in my studio, someone is gonna find the greatness in me."

Rick Lowe: Well and that is also connected to Jesse's theory. I remember that it was almost like they *had* to come to help us. Because if we did it by ourselves, it would have given us too much power. You want people to come around and to be involved and just do it. If you are doing it, then the rest of the world is not gonna let you do it by yourself because that is too empowering.

Bert Long: It reminds me of Chris Rock telling a joke: we don't have any black leaders, but we do have Al Sharpton and Jesse Jackson, and [Chris Rock] said, "Look over at Jesse Jackson, he went over there and got all those hostages." He said "When he got 'em, he told the people that were holding them, do you really want to make the USA mad? Let me have them."

(*Laughs*)

Thelma Smith: And it is true and the comments toward Jesse Jackson got worse and worse. After then, a lot of us, especially Black people, are a little anti-Jesse Jackson, but there has been so many negative things about him that it perpetuated itself.

Rick Lowe: And a lot of it manufactured.

Bert Long: He is very intelligent. You have to know that there is a glass ceiling. Chris Rock says: We talk one way when we are by ourselves and we talk another way when we are talking to them. You understand? I can't use the terminology that he used. An old man is talking to a Black person and is, "Yes Mr. Tom," by the time he turns back though, he says something else. So it is the same concept that we still face as artists right now. You know, my son says to me—as one of the young people these days that has an education, making the money, and everything—he wants to say, "Well, you went through bad times," and I said, "No. You have to understand that things still are not perfect."

Putting together this shoot: I am glad you did this. We need to have this. We are talking about other things like Mrs. de Menil and artists that are not here, but really it's at the core of where we are. Because we are not an island to ourselves.

Floyd Newsum: Mmm-hmm.

Bert Samples: Exactly.

Jesse Lott: Amen, brother.

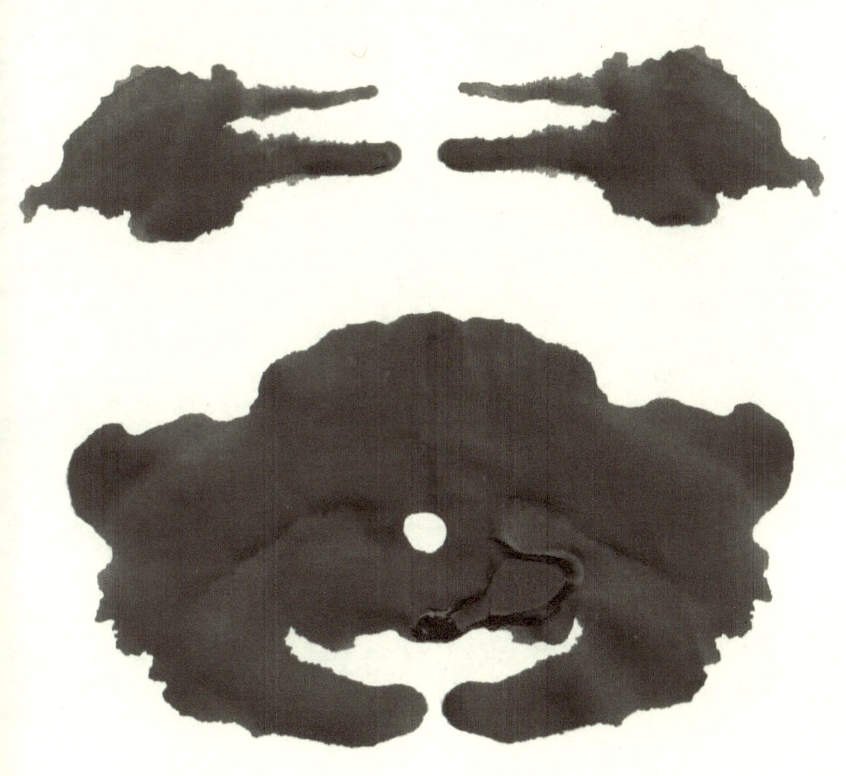

TALK AMONGST YOURSELVES

Nathaniel Donnett

Happy Thanksgiving! Entering the room, aroma of turkey, dressing, chicken

Thought bubble. It's grandfather's house. It's grandmother's house when grandfather's not angry.

Its an angry world. Family hugging, kissing, show love, asking my mom about my grades, but not asking me. I don't care, I travel silently to the back room and watch cartoons; so I thought. "Ahhhh mannnn, do I have to go in the front room?" I answered my mom, wondering if I'm going to be consumed by questions for me to dance the latest dance again. Oh well. My mother says, "Stay up here in the front for a little while, those cartoons ain't goin' nowhere." Thought bubble. Well, you all ain't either. I hear my cousins, going back and forth with each other. I take a breather, I don't realize at the time the damage of this conversation, but neither do they. Maybe its all about defining your conversation? Designing that conversation. Getting older, rewinding and teaching the youth by reminding them of that conversation.

"Hey black gal, give me some of that turkey." My cousin Mikel shouts, with a wide grin where you can only see his bright white teeth.

"Get your own, black boy" his sister, Tonya says. This obviously catches my attention. I ask Mikel about this exchange rather than Tonya, because Tonya seems like she can get angry and snap before Mikel will. So I figure asking him would rid me of any problems that I'm sure to be blamed for.

I ask, "Mikel, what's those names for? Why do you call her black gal and she call you black boy? You aint no boy, you like fifteen? You're a man right? Mikel replies, "Yep and
because cuz; we just playing and we both black. I tell my cousin, "I'm like dark brown or something like that, but ok." "Do you call Tanisha peanut butter" I ask. "She's the color of peanut butter."
Nah, we just call her Tanisha, or big head. "Oh okay" I said.

• • •

DR. DONNETT INTERVIEWS NATHANIEL: SESSION 1

Note: Client has been concerned about his issues with the word "black."

Dr. : Hello, sir, could you state your first name and initial?

N. : Nathaniel D.

Dr. : Thank you. So, what brings you here today?

N. : I've been having these dreams where I'm being picked on because of my skin color and it starts off by people calling me blackie. I don't know why, but I tell them I'm dark brown.

Dr. : What do you mean, and how have you been sleeping lately?

N. : Well, in school they call me these names. It starts off with blackie, then darkie, then things like tar baby. Stuff like that. I don't think its right nor do I think they realize they're being ignant; not ignorant, but ignant. I don't call people who look like me those names. My parents always talked about how being dark can hold you back and sometimes I believed them. It's like they became racists as a result of the racism they experienced.

Dr. : Hold you back from what?

N. : Well, things like jobs, dates, making it in the world.

Dr. : Well, maybe a long time ago that could happen, but I'm not so sure about that now.

N. : Hmmm. I was told by a few females that I was "too black," my hair was "too nappy," my nose was "too big," and I couldn't give them any "pretty babies."

Dr. : These sound like the types of ladies you wouldn't want in the first place.

N. : Doc, do you know who Puff Daddy is?

Dr. : Yes, he's the rapper, dancer, or he has a record label or something like that?

N. : Yes. He's all of those things. He's also a businessman who owns a vodka company. He put out a model call for his vodka ad and do you know the requirements? Women who were white, Hispanic or light-skinned African Americans. And by the way, I'm not a drinker, but it's still crazy.

Dr. : Are you kidding me?

N. : Nope! There's also the reggae singer called Vybz Kartel who lightened his skin and said something to the effect that black people can lighten their skin if they want to and if they want a different look. He said it's equivalent to whites darkening their skin. This happened in 2011.

Dr. : Oh my goodness. I have not heard of this.

N. : Also, that baseball player, Sammy Sosa, also lightened his skin too. I forget his reasons for it, but I'm thinking theres a color issue all around the world. I thought it was an old issue but I guess not. Anyway, maybe you're right doc. What do I know, other than I'm dark brown.

Dr. : Wow! I guess I stand to be corrected. Okay. Now, tell me about these dreams.

N. : Some are daydreams, some are at night. I keep seeing these shadows and they keep saying black, black, black, black! I go into an imaginary place when I have these dreams to feel safe. I also feel like i'm in a surreal place. I'm in this park where there are fifty foot African sculptures, books made of gold, slides and swings like one hundred feet tall, sometimes I'm able to fly away from them but usually I'm too frightened to do so.

Dr. : What you're having is called a Lucid Dream. That's when you know you're dreaming and know it's not real.

N. : Oh, okay. I see what you're saying. Thanks for that info Doc.

Dr. : Let's talk about your childhood. Did you have any friends in school?

N. : A few, but not many. I remember I always liked people that were different.

• • •

My bus is late, always running late. Running, running, running, and made it! "Thanks sir" The bus driver responds with a "No problem kid, you need to thank your friend. "I was about to
pull off, make these bus wheels spin." He said he saw you running. I dropped my coins in and headed to the middle of the bus; near my friend Kevon. I plopped in a seat in the middle. I don't like the front because you have to get out
your seat for the older ladies. I don't like to sit too
far in the back, because of those local crazies, plus Rosa Parks straighten out that part out like Madame CJ Walker, and I'm not trying to get burned or cut like hair at the
barber.
"Yo, Nate, I didn't think you'd catch the bus son,"
Kevon my good friend (I wonder why sometimes) is known for changing subjects, mid subject, amidst subjects, and asks me if I'm going to work.
Yeah man, gotta make that paper fare to get some new skater gear. He repeats, "Skater gear?"` "Man why don't you save up and get ya some Jordans."

Thought bubble. Kevon's into that slave wear. I laugh to myself.. Kevon likes to follow crowds, get mad macho. I can't be like Mike, only me. Thought bubble interruption with a Kevon subject change. Yo, Nate, check her out. She's fine huh?

Yeah. "Yo, Nate, she's got that good hair and light skinned." Yella, just like I like 'em." I'm like "Huh?" It doesn't matter
if they light skinned, dark skinned, good hair, or whatever." Even your conditioning is being conditioned. Man, you're darker than me and I'm dark brown.

"Nice looking and smart women is where its at." I try to
tell this fool, like Q-Tip said, "Black is Black." "I always
have to say that to keep Kevon's head straight.

Well "black" man, here's my stop, I'll catch ya later. Peace! Peace!

Running, running, running , to a time clock. "Ahem, excuse me Nathaniel do you have a watch, you're..." Oops, I say, its the assistant manager. Yes sir, sorry I'm late, but um..the bus was, um, um. That was dumb, dumb. My thoughts won't connect to my tongue, brain goes numb, numb.

"Well, Nathaniel, that's fine," says the assistant manger, "but the store manger is here and wants to speak with you."

Dang it. Working at Siesta is weird enough, some of the cashiers will start talking in code words. I suspect cold
words, hold words in captive prisms until they exonerate the old words from their prisons. Viva la freedom!

I don't need 'em. Walk towards the office. Sweat running, running, running down my forehead.. Knock on the door. Manager says come in, so I go ahead. The assistant manager comes in a few seconds slow. Iv'e read between these lines, seen these signs. These meetings are like corporate Rodney King beatings. Fired.

Montage of managers talking, you've been late, blah, blah, blah, I'm responding , but I'm in school, blah, blah, blah. their mouths are running, running, running...STOP! We have to let you go. I'm like say what? Stop! I'm gonna have to let
you know! I was gonna quit anyway. Stop! We'll need you to empty out your locker and take ya lock with you. At first
I started to play with them, say I don't understand, I don't
get you, I'm confused. Are you sure its not them, her, him
any of them? But then said its a waste. The store manger follows me to my locker and says, "You niggers never are on time." "Just a bunch of black niggers, dance, words, art and rhymes. "I'm like what the hell

did you say? Thought bubble. Don't do nothing, the cops are on their way. I say whatever, and never look back. I tell them to mail my check and

plus I'm dark brown, Bitches! Dang..the bus is comin..Running, running, running.

• • •

DR. DONNETT INTERVIEWS NATHANIEL: SESSION 2

Dr. : In the last session we talked about school and your youth. Tell me about what happened when you were not in school. How did you relax? Did you have any hobbies?

N. : Well, I didn't care for school much. I liked after school. I read comics and played drums. I liked visiting my family but would always resort to being alone.

Dr. : Why did you like playing music and could you elaborate?

N. : I was able to get some frustration out. I thought when I played music I was adding to the world, and communicating many stories old and new. The thing was that we could barely afford the drums. Before I had drums, I would beat on books, pots, and trashcans.

Dr. : Hmm, interesting. In the first session I remember you said you were called some negative names.

N. : Yes, um, darkie was one, tar baby is another. Stuff like that. The crazy thing about that was that the light-skinned people were called names too.

Dr. : How would you describe yourself?

N. : I'm dark-skinned, dark brown to be exact, medium height, bald, an overall nice guy.

Dr. : Well, Nathaniel, did you notice that when I asked you to describe yourself, that you did it from a physical perspective: you started with your skin tone, then moved inward to your personality?

N. : No, I didn't! Did I really? Wow. Really? Man, I'm as much a part of the problem as I blame others. That's funny because when I ask someone to describe someone to me, the first thing they will say is whether he or she is tall or short, big or small, light or dark skinned. Then they may get on my nerves and go into this "they got good or bad hair, because they got Indian in they blood" speech or something like that.

Both : Laughter.

Dr. : Interesting. Why do you think people do this?

N. : I don't know why. Tradition, lazy thinking, despair? I don't know really. Money? It always comes down to money. It also reminds me of music and words.

Dr. : What do you mean music and words?

N. : I mean, if you have words like blacklist, blackmail, black cat, and they mean something bad, why can't I make it mean something good?

Dr. : Go on.

N. : I noticed when you use certain language and words differently than how everyone else in society does, people view you as unintelligent. I think the media could be part of creating the stereotype, but people are guilty of believing it. I mean, like what we identify as black music, like soul, gospel, jazz, funk, rap, blues, and rap, they all use words and language in interesting ways. I don't considered that ignorance, I consider that to move language and words into a different space. Words from the rap generation have been recently placed in dictionaries and pop culture as the norm. I don't think its negative.

Dr. : I agree. I remember my mother telling me that it's a time and place for everything.

N. : I can agree with that too. My mama said the same thing. I figure if you have words like blacklist, blackball, blackmail and they're negative, why can't I change that into something positive?

Dr. : Give me an example.

N. : Like when I play music and it's good; why can't I call the process black? When I compliment someone, I can call it a black compliment. I look at what's going on now and then, and one thing seems to be true. I have the freedom to define things any way I want. I can define it. It doesn't have to define me in the negative, and black can be anything. It's up to me to see it differently.

Dr. : So you're saying an improvisation of words and self-definition against the negative portrayal or associations with the words black and black people?

N. : Um, yes. That sounds about right. (laughter) I'm just not interested in the division and negative characteristics applied to people for negative reasons. So I figure change it!

Dr. : So, in other words be the change you want to see in the world?

N. : Exactly! That's pretty good and deep doc.

Dr. : Thanks. I'd like to take credit, but it's a quote from Mahatma Gandhi.

N. : Well, I need to look him up. Sounds like something Dr. Martin Luther King would say.

Dr. : (Laughter) Yes, yes it does. So how do you feel now?

N. : I feel good, Doc. I was able to get some of the things in my head out. I appreciate you listening to me.

Dr. : Well, I appreciate you opening up to me and I enjoyed conversing with you as well. Sometimes we need to look at ourselves and within ourselves to find answers to our questions. Do you think you'll need any more sessions?

N. : I don't think so, Doc, but I feel great. I'm ready to go now, but I'll be back for more sessions if things haven't changed.

Dr. : You'll always be welcome, and that's very black of you; although I know you're dark brown.

Laughter.

TWO BUCKETS BACK EAST

Quincy Flowers

I hadn't thought about swimming or flying (or Sam neither) for a very long time, and had been staring out at the lake thinking about roasted peanuts. Maybe I had been getting ready to go for my shoes when a fully dressed man struggled out of the lake. He had difficulty there at the soppy bank, before the grassed part of it. Just as he reached the grass he fell against his knees and hands with his head dangling there, not lifting his gaze for some time. He did not rush to stand and look around him, he lingered until he had fully recovered. Half smiling when our gazes finally met.

I told him good evening when he was close enough, having spent the time watching him approach thinking about what I would say. All this was wrapped up in what he had come for and I had no guesses.

"You are here?" he said.

"Yes," I said, and looked around the veranda, which overlooked the valley, the lake below, the mountain tops opposite. "And now you here with me."

"Yep."

"Where you coming from?"

"That's why I'm here," he said. "I was in the city... and your name came up."

"Oh yeah?"

"Yeah."

I didn't say anything to that.

"I was having lunch with Uchefuna," he said.

I didn't say anything to that either but now he had me. Uchefuna. It had been a long time since I thought about her. I was a young man. No man at all—I was an old boy. By boy I mean to say that I was a sincere man. My friends and I thought that we would change the world. We thought that we could change the world. We believed in that. We all did. Every other day in the papers and on the tube young individuals and groups were standing up for something and making a little headway on this issue or that one. Sometimes toppling a hurdle altogether. Of course there were the instances where the papers and tube was showcasing individuals and groups getting their shit kicked in. But that was all the fuel we needed to feel that something must be done.

"She wants you to come," this man said to me and I immediately became suspicious. "She wonders why you gave up looking for her in the first place."

"Get out a here."

"What?"

"Uchefuna never looked for anyone... it doesn't work like that."

"That's exactly how it works." He stepped up to the highest level on to the veranda and sat in the other lawn chair, looked out to the valley. "What? You think it's people that look for her? And find her that way?" His mouth was flung wide now flashing baby teeth. "You don't believe that do you? You can't look for her if you tried."

"I tried."

"Well you can't succeed... you're right, you can try all you want. But like I just said you never find Uchefuna that way. She finds you. You sit there and she finds you."

"So what she say?"

"That's it," he shrugged. "She asked why you stopped looking for her, and I didn't know. Then she asked where you were, and I thought I'd look for you."

"How did you find me?"

This brought on his stony face, which he held for a second while looking me over. "You haven't been gone that long have you?" He said and I thought he must be kidding. His white teeth I could see in the low lit gloaming but otherwise would have taken him for toothless.

"Where were you thirty years ago?" I said, thinking about all of the times I had tried to explain or bring back the days, and becoming frustrated at that difficulty.

"What do you mean?"

"Don't worry a bout it."

He settled down then, seeming to take in the view for the first time though he had been looking in that direction. Then asked if I had come to this place in an attempt to look for Uchefuna and I told him that by the time I found this place I had given up on her long before. Those were my salad days, my foolish days, when not much was needed to stir the imagination. When a job proposal to sell knives that cut through a can of green beans door to door under the auspice of business manager had me walking around in the only blazer I owned, shirt and tied up with newspaper in tow. And to everyone in the neighborhood who asked what was up with the monkey suit I told them that they was looking at the next business manager. An exec ... who made his own hours and made his own work ... devised schemes and completed projects. I couldn't interpret their laughter my beam blinded me so. And definitely didn't believe Old Man when he said that he had seen the hustle before and that no one gave a non-degreed late-teen a job managing anybody's business, because it was exactly what the ad said they would do. And I had gotten an interview out of it. He didn't know anything is what I knew. That was in 1962. Things were way different than he remembered back before then. Plus I was in Detroit not the Canebrake.

But things don't change he said. It doesn't matter if it's 1922 or 1962 or 2012—things don't change. He also said that neither time nor place change the essential characteristics of life. Living is living. Make your own way, or sell yourself to the dogs to assist them in making theirs. He never said who the they and theirs were but I knew that all of it amounted to what I have always known as Old Man talk. After living with him you soon saw everything as a metaphor describing the good life on the farm he had created, the meals that got created as a result. None of his metaphors alluded to his children breaking their backs helping him create this.

In any case I hadn't been fifteen minutes on-the-job-training when I realized that the knife salesman slash business manager thing wasn't working for me, but the trainer had driven—and I hadn't the dime to hop a bus back to East Jefferson to quit properly, pick up my driver's license and other legal documents and then hop another bus home—and my trainer would lose too much time taking me back. So I watched him work for nine hours, hating every minute of it. It had nothing to do with managing business or executing crucial company decisions.

"My coming here," I told the man—"hey you want a towel or something? It's liable to get cold now the sun nearly down. The breeze'll pick up here shortly."

"No. I reckon be a waste of a towel since I'm going back through soon."

"Where you going now?"

"Back to the city ... I told you—I just came to find you. I'm here to tell you that Uchefuna asked about you, that she asked why you aint looking for her no more."

"I don't understand that ... can't say I believe it one bit."

"Well, it happened. I was right there just as sure as I'm sitting here talking to you."

I didn't say anything.

"I knew I had found you soon as I saw you up here looking at me—I knew it right away. But then I really really knew it when you aint have one bit of shock in your face at the fact I'm coming through the water to you. You had to be involved with the SBSC or one of the more antiquated sects from other parts of the globe that teaches the knowledge of flight and swimming to not budge the way you did."

I still didn't say anything. I still couldn't believe it. Uchefuna. I had only heard my sister Rita mention the name yet she couldn't explain how she had known about her because she said it wouldn't make any sense. "I will just say there's a beautiful lady by the name Uchefuna," Rita told me then. "That's all I'm a say. One day—soon as I get the knowledge of flight—I'm working on it, but soon as—I'll be gone and you'll know where I went."

When we were younger it was predestined that my own life be brought into company with those belonging to the Society of Brothers and Sisters and Children. Because of that conversation with my sister, I was able to answer, Uchefuna, when questioned about my desire to join by a leading figure in the Society. We were filing towards him, single row, and he, very efficiently and Messiah-like, said to each one, "Tell us why you want to walk with us?" When he got to me I said that I wanted to find Uchefuna, and walking with the Society could help with this, and he paused, as he had yet to interrupt his efficiency at responding to our answers with one of two words: granted or denied. Then, understanding the metaphor, he granted me passage to walk with the Society.

Though I hadn't thought about those days for years when this man stood wet from the lake, mentioning the name Uchefuna without warning and bringing it all back, the SBSC was the best thing that ever happened to me. To no avail I had spent years after my time with them trying to reconcile my prior ways of thinking about my life and the changes I had made to my life since those days. As far as reconciliation goes nothing I did helped put me in harmony with all things the way the days of walking with the Society had done. When the breaths turned over without effort. When I moved things around and saw the relationships of my thoughts and the physical world. I had lost all of those abilities and not even moving to this cabin at the edge of the valley that overlooked the bowl of reflection had brought them back. Where I used to swim to places and now a man had come through to tell me something. Yet I was suspicious. Though it was the kind of suspicion that is soon turned over to another, stronger intuition, I told the man with a full set of baby teeth that I had no desire to rekindle my trek for Uchefuna. "Those days behind me now."

"I see," he said unaffected.

"Well?"

"Well. I guess that's that." He stood then and dipped his head while holding his eyes on me before returning to the lake.

For days all I could think about was this man. And Uchefuna. I had come to have a routine during the late spring season that included sitting out on the veranda several times a day, but with the man and Uchefuna on my mind things were off. Bad enough I'd think about her before bed, dream about her, and all throughout the house as I carried out my business, looking out over the lake no longer meant sitting with my tea or a beer and roasted peanuts until I lost track of myself.

It was about three days shuffling around the house like this before I decided to visit Peebo. He wasn't home. His wife let me in, saying that Peebo had gone into town but would be back before long. She wanted to know why I had stayed away so long. Said that she couldn't believe I hadn't gone crazy in that great big old house all by myself and no one to laugh with, remembering old good days at the least.

"Ah, you know," I said, "how I am. "I'm my own good company."

"You just old." She coughed out a laugh.

"We all old."

"That's why I know it's the age—it's that worn body of yours and aint got nothing to do with you not needing any company."

"How you and Peebo making out?"

"We all right on this side. Just getting ready for the grandkids this summer."

I didn't say anything

"What's the matter?"

"Ah, nothing," I said looking around at the den and old timey furniture in it.

"Well, don't mind me, I'm a get back to working in this other room here, the work got a be completed by Monday and I don't see how." I didn't say anything to that but watched her move away, seeming when she turned, concerned, maybe believing I had come to ask for something.

Peebo walked in singing. He had started to say something and caught himself when he realized that it was me in the den.

"I was just about to say—I thought you was Daphne. What's going on?"

"Ah, nothing."

"Daphne talking about she aint want to be bothered today because she got her lecture to write and I thought she was in here relaxing or something."

"No, she was here talking with me when I come in, but went back there to work. She did say she was strapped about it."

"Yeah, she's strapped." He pulled a Löwenbräu out of the bag and offered it to me.

"Sure"

"How things down your way?" he said, popping the bottle top off.

"They alright."

"Yeah," he said, "I see you up for long walks."

"I guess," I said, and was about to leave it at that but decided to tell him that I needed to think about things and that it was an in-the-moment urge to walk that hit me just as I unlocked the car doors with my key ring. Then I told him about the man who had come through the lake three days before to tell me that Uchefuna was asking about me."

"Get out a here."

"That's what I told him"

"That's what I'm telling you."

"What?"

"You serious?"

"As a heart attack."

"Damn ... Uchefuna?"

We let the silence between us hang there for a moment, understanding that each of us had come a long way from the Society of Brothers Sisters and Children days. Peebo glided his palm over the patch of bald on the top of his head, again and again, like he was combing it. I took several gulps of beer down as I watched him become me three days prior. He knew about Uchefuna through me. She was not the object of his walk with the SBSC. When asked why he wanted to journey with them, Peebo had told them that he wanted to find buried treasures. I told him he'd never get in if he told them that but he insisted that they already knew our hearts, and that the question was more a test of honesty than anything else. To my surprise one of the leaders holding initiation hearings the day Peebo was on the line granted him acceptance into the Society, saying that if it was treasures he sought, he'd find all the riches he could never imagine.

Peebo asked me what I would do. He said that if it was true, if Uchefuna was really looking for me that I should go to her. He wished someone would come through to tell him that his treasure was looking for him and I nearly spit out my beer to keep from choking. "I wish," I said, "the man would have told me that." Peebo laughed with me. "You got enough. You and Daphne got three homes so I don't know what you talking about."

"I'm talking about these three homes is eating my ass up. I can't keep up with anything and doesn't make sense to have three of everything. If it was up to me I wouldn't have but one place to live."

"Which one?"

He didn't say anything.

"See," I said to him, knowing he was just as responsible for his multiple homes as Daphne. He loved it here in the valley. Peaceful in the valley. Plus it was coming through that lake that led us to this place. But the home in Paris was spectacular, and kept him active, both because it was physically demanding being in the midst of everything and he was forced to learn French. Daphne was fluent and tried as best she could to help him get there, but he had depended on her to handle all of their affairs while in France.

Some weeks passed. I still could not shake the thought of Uchefuna but it had gotten a lot better. It was not constant, just hit me now and again. Someone rang my bell and when I went to the door the man who had come through the lake was standing there, wet again. I let him on in. He reminded me why I had learned to fly as well as swim, watching him drip over everything, considering whether I should invite him all the way in. "Take your shoes off," I told him. "Come through this way and wait in the kitchen."

When I returned with a towel he was standing there naked, his clothes on the floor in a pile. "Dry off with this here," I said. "Should I dry those for you?"

"That would be good. I don't plan to stay long though."

"Well at least let these dry and have something hot."

"That would be good," he said again. He dried with the towel and when done with that wrapped it around him and sat at the table. He said that Uchefuna wanted to see me; that she thought for sure once I knew she had asked about me it would motivate me to set out for her again.

"Does she know that I am seventy-two years old now, that it's not 1962 anymore?"

He didn't say anything

"Why don't you fly here?"

"Excuse me?"

"Aren't you uncomfortable sitting in my kitchen with a towel wrapped around you like you at the sauna?"

"No, I'm fine, thank you. Just came to relay this message and I'll be on my way. Are you coming back with me," he said. "Uchefuna would like it if you came back with me. You are a dinner guest tonight."

I didn't say anything.

"You don't have to stay long—just dinner."

The rain cloud was making its way over the mountains when I was watching him go. I told him that I had already had dinner plans but would come tomorrow, asked also if I could bring friends and he said that he would see. When he returned tomorrow he would let me know what Uchefuna thought about it.

Peebo was sleeping when I rang his bell and answered the door in an old t-shirt and his drawers. He squintched his eyes and jerked his neck back when I mentioned that I had had enough of looking at dicks today. I told him about the man sitting in my kitchen butt-ass naked sipping tea like it was alright. And then told him about the dinner invitation.

"Where does Uchefuna stay," he wanted to know.

"I don't know. This guy say he and her meet up in the city. But I don't know. Don't even know if he means New York. You know?"

"So you going?"

"If you and Daphne come with me."

"Daphne at a conference and won't be back till Thursday."

"Even better—you should come then."

He chewed on that for a while and then said sure, he wasn't doing anything else. He had fought the idea of marrying Daphne for years but in time couldn't take her being away too long.

When the man had come through the lake the next day he was disappointed that he had to tell me Peebo could not come. Uchefuna wanted to meet with me. At some other time, she would meet my friends.

"I won't go then," I said. Then I told him I regretted his having to come all the way just for it to go down like this. "Maybe if my friend come anyway she won't mind?"

"Suit yourself," he shrugged. "But I told you what she said."

It struck me in that moment that this Uchefuna, supposedly the most beautiful creature ever born, must be very old. She was already a mature adult in my mind as I searched for her as a youth, and that was fifty and odd years ago.

It took Peebo an hour to arrive. Once there he and I argued about whether he should go or not. It was a restaurant I tried to tell him, and who was to say if he was allowed to dine or not. Maybe she doesn't want him sitting at the table, I explained, and maybe she wouldn't pay his ticket, but he didn't need her to. Neither one of us did. The man stood there swinging his eyes from one of us to the other while we went at this and finally, when it was settled, I went for my buckets in the garage.

"What are you doing?" the man said when I returned.

"Are we not going to the city?" I was looking at him then, with my hands pointed in his direction as if he was about to throw me something. And he looked at Peebo and Peebo shrugged. I started filling the buckets with water then.

"Ok," the man finally said. "I'll meet you there. Do you need directions?"

"No. It's been a long time but I will find it. I will find the place."

"Ok," the man said again. "See you there."

"See you there." And I sat the buckets together, rolled up my pant legs and stepped in.

I went first and told Peebo that I would wait for him to come through, and landed on the top of a building overlooking the East River and the Watchtower Building in the Heights. It shouldn't have taken Peebo long to trail me, but I thought I'd walk to the edge of the rooftop and take in that view, considering how bizarre the feeling of spectacular views were. I wondered was the same feeling elicited when I looked over the lake and the mountaintops because it sure felt similar enough. When one says spectacular view is it the same spectacular every time? Even looking up the river towards the Chrysler Building I wondered was I witnessing the same spectacular as I witnessed the last time I set my eyes on the city's lines. When I used to live in Brooklyn I could never not be awed by those lines, as omnipresent as they are, any time I rode across the Manhattan Bridge or turning the bend on the BQE coming from LaGuardia.

I lost track of time looking around the place yet knew without a doubt that Peebo should have arrived by then. Thinking that he had changed his mind, telling myself that I would give him a little longer before I went out for Uchefuna. I waited and I waited but Peebo never showed. It came to me then that this dinner was not at a restaurant at all but at Uchefuna's home, and then it came to me that I should head uptown on an eastside train. It was a good feeling since it had been a very long time ago that knowing something had occurred for me in this way—dropping in there in the quietude of thinking, or better yet not thinking at all, or at least not being aware of the thought, as had been the case standing on the rooftop looking out.

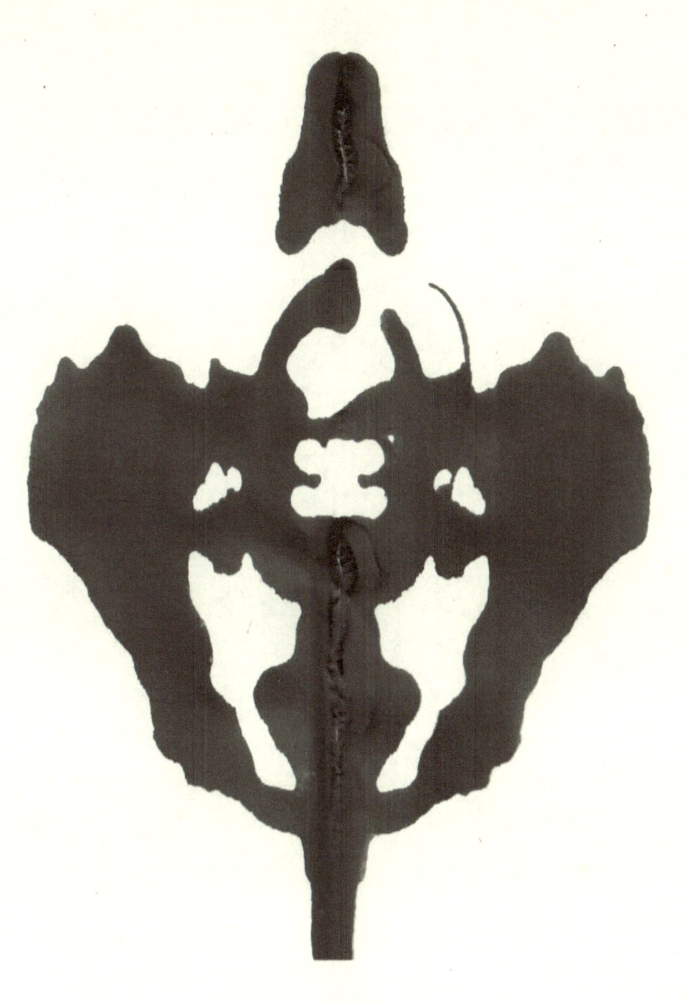

WHEN THE PAGE HITS THE FAN

Michael Kahlil Taylor

Houston was filled with open mics and poetry slams like never before in 2004, three venues in a single night, but I rarely "read" because my written work didn't translate to a stage verbally. Trying to figure out how I could use metaphor and alliteration on a stage was a challenge. I began learning the rules and culture of spoken word performance and poetry slam: being judged by five "random" people from the audience, three minute time limits, lowest score eliminations.

Unlike academia where teachers offer every student an opportunity to share with the class, open mics in Houston were competitive. Slots on the sign up lists were limited and hosts would put poets up in any order they thought would build momentum based on crowd response, and when there was overflow the hosts would have to choose who could perform and who would have to wait. If I wanted to share the ideas of that day I'd need to be "better" than another name on the list or all the passion, patience and desire for dialogue about the subject would be wasted on sidewalk conversations outside. I'd have to learn something very different from the safety of an audience reading and re-reading within the comfort of their home, I'd have to learn how to "slam" a poem in one listen with the background noise of a bar or comedy club.

When struggling to memorize poems I could only remember the idea of about two lines before not having a clue what came next, until I started memorizing visually and rhythmically. I'd grown up on hip hop during the original *Yo! MTV Raps* and *Rap City* era. All the poems/raps I already knew had videos. So I began writing poems that I could visualize line for line and as I began performing them the natural rhythm of the words would develop into a pattern. As the videos became sequenced in my memory I was able to memorize some of the words and look at the audience for "live feedback." The audience became a critique of every phrase and word which helped me realize whether or not I was communicating clearly. Like my hip hop freestyle days, when we would make up raps about our surroundings while simultaneously reciting the line, I began editing my poems on stage removing words and phrases that didn't work until each non-essential word was eliminated, which meant less words to memorize.

Each time I looked at a poem on the page it would seem more foreign because I had changed the delivery on stage and now remembered something different from the page. Performance poetry had a completely different set of dynamics than written poetry. Consonance, alliteration, metaphors and similes were only as valuable as their ability to clearly communicate an idea under the restrictions of breath control and room volume. I'd take a passionate idea, write it as technical poetry, trim the poem to half its size through repeat performance, and rebuild the poem based upon the audience's emotional response during the performance. The poems were being judged by the last feeling an average person had at the end of listening, the result of a connection created in less than 3 min. Success meant an opportunity to perform again but failure to communicate would leave me in the audience observing what I had not achieved.

I began focusing on listening to both the audience and my own natural rhythms and subconscious physical movements to re-write my poems for performance. Then I also began developing notations and notes to help me memorize what had most often been born onstage hoping the combination of all the aspects of performance would help me actually memorize the words. I never quite managed to memorize the exact words but I finished the films inside my head and learned how to communicate big ideas with the least amount of words by transforming paragraphs into stanzas. I am currently putting performance poems back onto the page and working to write poems that work equally in both environments.

Notation: The first two poems "Every Conversation" and "Tear Drops" are performance scripts with notation notes for voice fluctuation and movement. Each notation is within parenthesis and most often written in a vowel-less abbreviation influenced by my earlier exposure to Tetragrammaton and ciphers. Some examples are slw=Slow, ps=Pause, nd=End, and hgh=High Volume. The remaining poems are performance works that were later laid on the page for a reading audience.

* *Previous versions of "Every Conversation" and "Silent" were published in an eight handmade edition book sold at the 2005 National Poetry Slam along with "Dreamcatcher" which has remained unchanged.*

EVERY CONVERSATION (2005)

(Strtng pose "almost lotus" or standing cross position)

I stand before god and his face looks familiar (slw+ps)
Now I finally understand (ps)
That every conversation I ever had with anyone including myself (nd hgh)
was simply a conversation with him (switch the regular stand position)

And now words are inked into my tongue like skin tattoos (fcs "s" on sound)
shifting into position for exposition like the illustrated man (shftng bdy mvmnts)

And words

Words leap out my heart like blades of grass breaking through concrete streets refusing to believe that even solid granite (fst + hrd-"leap" "break" "granite"+ps)

is strong enough to keep them from reaching the sun (slw)
from reaching god

and a simple glass of tea is an ocean of inspiration (fcs + drg "ocean")

while I patiently wait for words to lay down their lives like soldiers on the front lines (fst trns)

Yes Truth is contagious (hrd+ps+hrd+fstfst)
Yes The media is an anti-virus (fst)
So I refuse their serum

And sleep blanketed by words from old folks at homeless park benches, bus stops, and everyday casual conversations (fst)

Every conversation I ever had with anyone including myself (fst+nd hgh+ps)
could have just been a conversation with him (slw)
a conversation with you (slw, point at individual in audience)
a conversation with her (slw, p.i.a.)
a conversation with god (slw, p.i.a)

So now I talk back to the wind when it delivers divine inspiration (hgh "wind")
then whistle (ps)
Vedic Biblical Koran Hieroglyphic born scriptures that will enter the ears of birds flying to foreign continents where some young child will hear that bird's whistle and suddenly have a revelation of their truth (ps)

(walk into crowd and finish poem speaking directly to audience)

I could walk through hell barefoot only armed with this poem (fst+hrd)
and speak words to the devil so sincere that lost souls could be redeemed (fst)
borrow words from the divine so powerful that monks all the way in Tibet would be the echo (ps)

Why fear death? (ps)
It's just life ... (ps)
without flesh (hgh)

It's where we come from
Where we'll be going
Our skin is just a costume
We are all actors in the exact same play just searching for the plot (global size gesture)
And there is a purpose to it all whether we understand him or not

So I stand on the shoulders of all the poets before me climbing Jacob's ladder to reach an elevated state of rhyme (ladder climbing movements, ps)

Running this track meet with god in full faith (fst)
reaching for the baton but never once looking behind (fst, arm reaching back)
Understanding our voice is his and our bodies his pantomime (ps)

Because ...
I died already. (clm+ps)
The day I watched my mother's tears roll down her face because the words coming out of my mouth didn't not reflect hers (clm)
I cried (ps)
because no matter how many words my mother spoke it could not change my purpose (fst+fst)

And my mother's words laid (fst+ps)
heavy on my mind like (fst+ps)
Gabriel's bloody body draped over the back on Michael's angelic warrior wings (ps, back arched up as if carrying weight)
But my war in heaven (ps)

Is a daily battle where metaphors pick up swords against similes fighting for the revelation of which one I'll speak first (fst+hrd)

There is only you, (slw+clm)
you (pnt at indvdul, rpt rpt rpt)
you
and god
and god
and god
and god (rtrn to stge)

So every conversation you every have with anyone including yourself...
Could just be a conversation with her. (point toward the sky suggesting genderless god)

So now the questions of the moment are these (rtrn to strt position variation)

Are we sitting in a room of human beings or angels (flw)
Am I standing as a physical reality speaking (ps+qstn)
or are we all just a vision inside your head (ps+qstn)
and you're having a personal conversation (lng ps)
with him

• • •

TEAR DROPS IN ORBIT (2003)

(each lne hs ps, slw poem)

And as her tear drops
Kissed her grandmother's forehead
She
Rose from her knees
and turned to face a world
That her twelve-year-old eyes had never seen before

And walked through the rubble of
splintered wood
broken concrete
and stain-glassed memories

newly crowned memories that
she would have to wear embroidered under her skin
and draped under her daily garments
And maybe

(str stnza fast nd slw)
Maybe the loss of her hearing after the last bomb blast was really a blessing
Because now she could only see
People with their mouths wide-open and eyes tightly shut
but she does not suffer the sounds of their screams (s s s s fcs)
or the sirens that seem (s s fcs)
to be never ending

colored fluids like blood and urine that usually hide on the insides of people
now freely flow as a stream across the sand streets

(str stnza fast nd slw)
she knows that for some things in life
god offers no rational explanation
So she didn't bother asking

She just stares into the night sky
Awed by the auras that brighten it
Hoping to wake up in any real world other than this
she soon falls asleep in the dark corner of a soon-to-be bombed building

(str stnza fast nd slw)
And four hours after the bombs dropped
a soldier walks by
Protected by
camouflaged cloth armor
But nothing can protect his conscience
as he looks and sees the eyes of girl
a little girl whose eyes look like a daughter he faintly remembers
one who he does not claim

(str stnza fast nd slw)
One who
three weeks later
sits still in history class
staring at the glass screen
wondering why the yellow face of a P.O.W. soldier
looks like a father she faintly remembers

A father she will wish was there to (spc the wrds aft "is")
beat and bag the boys who (nd spc)
rape her in the school restroom

a father she will wish is just there to (spc the wrds aft "is")
hold her hand

as she sits in the principal's office
failing to explain and prove her rape to an ex-military man
who can see no wrong
because once
he was at war with himself
his god
his still segregated nation
but killing Asian men he had never had a reason to hate
Men whose name he couldn't even pronounce
men who did less to hurt his people
than those who lynched, burned and bagged them
daily

(str stnza fast nd slw)

Remembering past days when,
whatever ship's dock he stood on,
Standing there in full uniform,
unified by an enemy he was still
a Nigga

Going home just to turn on the T.V. and
not to see his son die in the hands of those
"Sand Niggas"
"Sand Niggas"
"Sand Niggas"
Turning on the same T.V. just to see his son standing in front of the
exact same commander who had once called him a Nigga

(fnsh slw)
This young man
flies an airplane destroying a military target
near residential houses
building falls into pieces
one rock
one atomic pebble
falls through the roof of a building
killing an entire family
leaving a little girl crying over her grandmother

At this point in the poem
I the poet
begin to wonder
if anyone in the audience is wondering why I wrote this.
I wrote it because I can't stand for it
So I stand at mics and share it

Sometimes we poets act like reality with responsibility doesn't exist

I find myself writing love poems
to console the broken hearts of love poets

who now only write love poems to get sex from girls we never intend to offer love

(str stnza fast nd slw)
I find myself wanting to write "revolutionary"poems
against"revolutionary"poets (srcasm tond "rvlution")
whose personal live are so messed up with crimes against their own
I couldn't trust them with my sister ... much less a nation
(replace "sister" with "daughter" to mask having a younger sister if needed)
But that's a poem for another time
and this poet who just hopes to contribute to peace through poetry
has one last word ...
"peace"

FALLING UP (2010)

walking backward at times
not seeing next   a pretext   for rediscovery
moonwalking on a comet   roadrunning in rewind
invisible to telescopes   outer space within the mind
unwrapping impossible   believe slightly too much
a creative perpetual klutz

strolling off the edge of the world and falling off
but falling   up

rediscovering gravity might be tough
so what   now
space is the place   arrived too late

alone
amongst galaxies

sum of humankind   caught in rewind
reversing verse
a theory   banging   big
falling too far

sun ra shel silvestein invisible ellison rita dove gibraning shooting star
outer space within the mind   never far

clearly   nuclear   blackwhole
created creator creation
inner-space station
mediated meditation

discovering   confidence   recovering
illusion of   grounding reality   antigravity
slightly   hovering   craft

reflect   tcelfer
walking was impossible   born day   initial contact

set against a wall   imagined a crawl
followed a vision   finally walked tall

Impossible   unlearn
Infinite   relearn

this moment   shaping eternity   future present

when in retrospect   one satirical laugh
failures of past   just   grandchildren of future success

heavyweight imagination   meteor to end an ice age
no longer frozen

chose   to   create

SILENT (2005 performance / 2011 edited for page)

i want to stuff child molesters with m16 rifles
and blast holes through their hearts
that exit their heads

and even if i hung him from a tree
right below his balls
until the weight of his own body
broke it   off
I would still
    not feel
        redeemed

don't talk to strangers is a simple phrase that never came with any
real explanations
so imagine   or   don't imagine

a young boy holding hands with a man he doesn't know will touch
him in places god had not yet matured
sexuality was a question for half a life

no doctor
mother   too   ashamed
so doctor never told me I wasn't alone
or society failed to protect me like thousands of other boys who would
never   make the statistics

painful enough words have not yet been created
lest the definitions be too painful to print

colors replaced words as i drew on sheets my teacher gave me after
school just so i wouldn't have to go home early
she wasn't so busy marking papers that she could not see the marks
in my eyes
                        when suddenly
         a straight-A student came to school

silent

i had been trained to never tell secrets
every morning i would hide them in the small pocket of my jeans
hoping they would fall out unnoticed when i paid for lunch

hungry
but afraid to eat
because I could not stand anything
                                              inside
me

this is not my poem
it's the testimony of thousands

it's two suicidal little boys sitting on the stoop hugging each other
because they share secrets
their mother will never know

it's the smell

of stained carpets in little boy's rooms
socks muffling screams so as not to be heard
mothers who aren't really asleep
crying

listening but still selling souls of their children
exchanging for
attention   drugs   whatever the fuck
she thought could make her feel better
about herself

the boy doesn't know that she knows
and doesn't want daddy to leave her alone again
so in the morning during breakfast
they all sit at the table
nothing to eat but

silence

the sunday school teacher not speaking about
eyes of boys exiting pastor's office
on saturday afternoons

she would hate
for it to cast a shadow over the church

god will sort it out

as if god wasn't commissioning her to act for him
as if all those sunday school scriptures
weren't just lessons telling her that the savior lies
within

if this poem sounds harsh
like images inserted   into your head   unwillingly
in a place you don't feel comfortable
unmovable emotions trapped inside your mind
stuck inside ours
so that the moment we see something that doesn't look right

you will   stop

find out what happened

it's just that important

may we all
be no longer

silent

ORIGAMI BUTTERFLY

(2005 performance, 2011 edited for page)

and so
a few mornings after

awakened from a dream
wanting to make u an origami butterfly

that evening
unsuccessfully attempted to recreate one
now experience pulp for future paper
but enjoyed the process

so
sitting and reprocessing
peaceful memories that
will continue unfolding forever
while still creased firm within a moment

the past was
just a dusty mirror cracked with reasons
polished with future plans justifying why not

but that moment
restrained caution

that moment
unfolded within arms
formed in two a
free expression
creased and caressed folds

a lion mained with disillusioned experience

beats miscued heart
heart beats miscued
miscued heart beats

now
finger tip pressuring
embellishment evident

a new rhythm
in places special things once folded closed
still thrive with
colors visible only to touch

a metamorphic dance between creased
elegant lion butterfly wings
flapping in a breeze
childlike chasing a butterfly across field
catching elusive imagination

later

our morning sun rose
clear window
no reflection
dilated pupils reflecting a fleeting moment
fading dyes and hues
creaseless
unembellished
unfolded

DREAMCATCHER (2005 performance and page)

as a child Richard Oakes used to call Me
a Dreamcatcher
because his daughter Yvonne was the best dream I ever caught.
the time was 1969
and we were Native Americans
reclaiming the abandoned prison island of Alcatraz as our new battle line

UCLA American-Indian Students and 80
80 natives from tribes across this nation
patiently worked with our leader and Yvonne's father Richard Oakes
the Mohawk Indian whose dreams   would give us hope
to both   me and he
Yvonne was our metaphor of dreams to be
as me and she rewrote history
with poem graffiti on the prison that had become our pyramid playground
laughing
laughing at the irony of our people being relocated to land reserved
as if Native People actually had reservations to get land back at some time

but maybe
maybe Land Reservations were just used to keep us preserved
preserved as a great conquering reminder
of what rewards theft and carnage can bring

maybe their scalping our heads would make us forget our history
maybe history had wrapped around our necks strangling our dreams
like small pox blankets used as a nooses to create fear

despite it all   Yvonne and I played here.
underneath torn whistling barbed wire
running around the prison shooting like Indians and Cowboys
remembering a history quite different than the ones in our
used by others then thrown away to us five years behind the present
history books.

as if we should only be concerned with the past
as if we need not bother with knowledge of politics in the present
or the future

so we learned history while listening on the Alcatraz coast
she loved poetry the most
now I sit and reread my notes about our hopes and Dreams.

but my hopes and dreams
died
the day Yvonne died
things
don't seem to mean as much
we
don't seem to care as much
things
change like the only constant is change so
guess that's why I constantly think
of the shades of her beauty as the Sun Shone through the Leaves.
and her Father would seem to fall apart once Yvonne fell like those leaves
I would watch a nation die with the last drum of her delicate heart beat
feet beat
the sands of Alcatraz as Dreamcatchers surrounded her like a fallen angel
and time stood still like we all stood still
staring as Oaks left the island with Yvonne's body
never to return again like our dreams never returned again

President Nixon never interfered with the world-wide publicized occupation
because who cares
about what an abandoned prison island used to be to us back then
when
the F.B.I. arrived in 1971 there were only 15
Natives left to defend,
the dreams of the original 80 that had been caught up in the wind.

and screaming spirits cried as our dreams were captured
and dreaming after became illusions stuck in plaster
& I became the voice of my ancestors past.
hoping children will do poem graffiti smoke signals in schools,
to fill their history class with a true but often untold well
forgotten American past.

DISSIDENT

Ayanna Jolivet McCloud

the
economy
of
my
body
rejects
the
motions
that
my
nation(s)
pull
me
towards.

the
pull
at
the
core
of
the
Earth
rejects
the
rhythm
that
my
nation
pulls it
against.

it is a
counterintuitive
motion
that
moves
against
the
grains
of
a
life
with
borders
and
names
for names

if
measuring
my
internal
rhythm
and
the
nervous
flattering
of
my
eyelashes
or
the
irregular
beating
of
my
heartbeat
or the
pointed
and
violent
language
i
pose
against
my selves,

then

i am
a
dissident
in my own
body.

INSTRUCTION MANUAL.*

Ayanna Jolivet McCloud

1. Live Multiply. Live many lives, many times over. Disrupt your single self. Allow a chasm to break you into itty bitty pieces. Embrace gaps. Allow fragile lines to become deep cracks. Pursue openings made by disruption. A cleft. A fissure. A wide and deep break. Erect borders that allow your selves to stand firm. And dissipate. And be born again with each fleeting moment. **2. Run.** Be incredibly adaptable by necessity. Move quickly. Leap through the forests and trees. Hear the echoed memories of strange fruit. Which hang limply from their limbs. Allow their spirits to trip you and hug you tightly. Refuel. Run through deep circles of wind that give breath to tiny hurricanes. Know these will crush you and may break you. **3. Remember.** When color was a stain. The blanket whiteness of the arctic, year nineteen zero nine. You are engulfed by small, steep mountains of ice, great sheets of crushing cold. A body you cannot feel. Your footsteps proceed you. You are the first to reach the North Pole. Your name is Matthew Henson. You are a cabin boy, then a seaman, always an explorer. Recall but know that you will be forgotten. There will be others. **4. And Forget.** Today is simply the day after yesterday and the day before tomorrow and yesterday is the day before today and the day anticipating tomorrow and the past gives birth to the future but the future is indebted to the past and the present is compressed by the future and periods before. **5. And Imagine.** Locate your blackness like the whale with three eyes or the minotaur with spiraled horns or the unicorn with metallic hooves. It will and can be as real as you imagine it. **6. Un-Name.** Move beyond your objecthood. Place truth not in the outline. But when the borders collide. Giving birth to the negative space that becomes your islands. Live where boundaries collide and exist no more. **7. Vanish.**

* For Isaih, Trenton, Ebony, Sidney, Malcolm (and Datron)

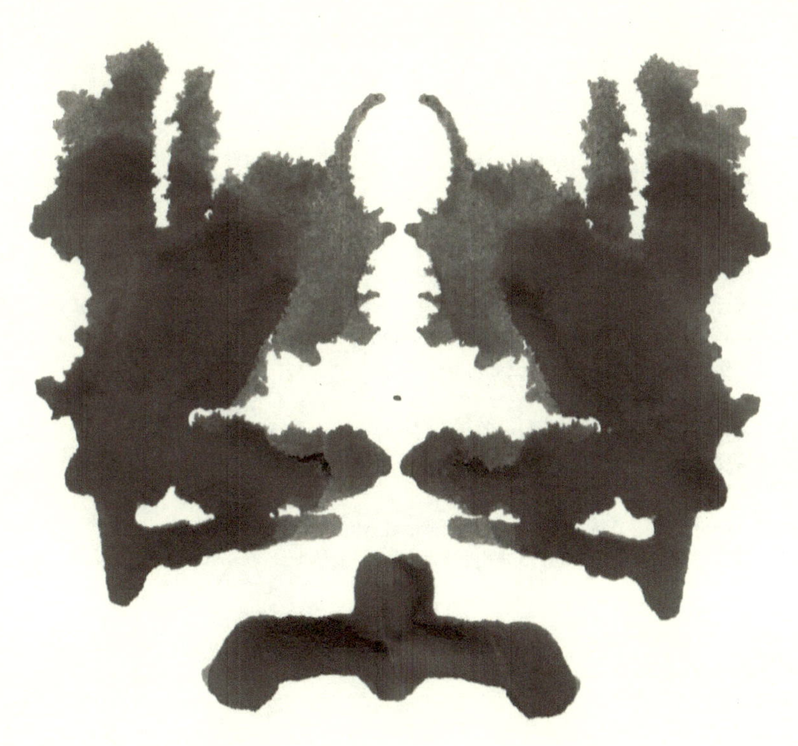

OTHER: FROM NOUN TO VERB

February 9, 2011

One month after the first roundtable, Book Club invited The Marvelous Six to join us in a reading and conversation. The evening followed our conventional format: we began with a reading, and the subsequent discussion evolved into a conversation about our work, the histories that influence us, and new possibilities for the future.

Nathaniel Mackey's essay "Other: From Noun to Verb,"* served as the starting point for our conversation that day.

Because the discussion was informal, the players have been anonymized. Here are some highlights:

---

* Mackey, Nathaniel. "Other: From Noun to Verb." *Representations* 39 (Summer 1992): 51–70

- - I always forget that we've been so deeply studied for so long. I'm fascinated by the idea that white people were trying to study "How did you make that musical note?" and weren't able to deconstruct it then. I wonder if now they have deconstructed it well enough to produce an [Christina] Aguilera, or is it still just mimicry?

- - Remember in *White Men Can't Jump* when he still wouldn't hear Jimi? And that was in the '90s?

- - I think it is interesting to see the repetition of parallels. A friend of mine is a DJ. I don't listen to a lot of the music that comes out now, but I hear it when I hang out with him. He played this series of songs for me and I asked him, "What is this stuff?" and he was like, "Man they're making money." But the definition of "making money" was essentially mimicry of stuff that black people had traditionally suffered for. They were called names to speak that way; they were categorized in ways such that they couldn't make money if they continued doing that; they were marginalized. And now all of these things that rap artists and R&B artists suffered through for a decade plus are now popular and now other people can do the exact same things they suffered for without any real penalty. I think that's something I've been able to see in my time is people who suffer to be able to say certain things or have certain freedoms, even to be improper in a sense. In reading this, "improper" is not just improper but sometimes it's a rebellion against what's proper. It's not "ignorance," it is creating something contrary to what is considered normal.

- - For instance, like that Eminem commercial for the Super Bowl. Did everybody see that? It was a Claymation thing with him just totally hip hop bravado and stuff using profanity through the commercial to sell tea and stuff like that.

- - Speaking of the Superbowl: Justin Timberlake. You know that moment where he got into that situation with Janet Jackson. Janet took all the heat. I really had a higher level of respect for Britney [Spears] when she shaved her head. That's cool. I saw her in a new light for five minutes. I would have had a new appreciation for Timberlake if he would have taken that heat. Because it's that heat that allows him to make the music that he makes, you know? I think it was a bad move on his part to just step away from her and act like he didn't have anything to do with the opportunity to share a black person's heat.

- - Can some one maybe explain, I'm a little confused about this "artistic othering" and "social othering." I know that is how he starts out, I was wondering if someone understands what that means. Because the last sentence in the first paragraph says "my focus is the practice of the former by people subjected to the latter," so it seems like it's a very important lead into the text. I was wondering if someone could clarify this "artistic othering" and "social othering."

- - I think that with "artistic othering," he is referring to the idea that creating art is essentially changing existing ideas. Since all we have to work with is what already exists it's "making strange" existing material, "making new," existing material and in making new it's also unfamiliar. At least that's the way I understood it. By "othering," in both cases, he's talking about making something unfamiliar or unusual in order for it to be experienced in a different way. In "artistic othering that's a positive thing, but in social othering that a negative thing: making something unfamiliar or alien in order for it to be less approachable.

- - In reading that and thinking about the usage of hip-hop slang, when he says "artistic othering has to do with innovation and invention," those things happen because they relate to the area that person grew up in, they kind of form from the way that people live life and at that time it was artistic othering, but then those exact same things would get labeled as ebonics and then society would then use it do a social othering like they speak different. That is social othering, and then when you talk about a popularity thing that which was social othering is now artistic when someone else does it. So when Eminem does it that's artistic, that's inclusive because he gets credit for being innovative or creative.

I think we go through that difference where we're doing it artistically to create something but then society says that something other than us and then when they're ready to embrace it it becomes artistic to them doing it, but when we did it we were put out for it. And when they do it then it's creative now instead of having just ... before it was just some other stuff, now it's creative but it's the exact same thing.

- - I think about repetition and how now it seems like you have laws, like copyright laws that really kind of prevent the natural progression of a tradition which before had existed for years and years. For instance, "versioning," where someone is doing several different takes of a particular song is now a lot more difficult than it used to be.

- - Copyright laws are so not static, it seems. They evolve so much in response to the kind of challenges they face. It's interesting thinking about how copyright laws are constantly under pressure by activities of artists who push against them and so often artist find ways legally, slightly illegally, more illegally to push the law, change the law so that creative practice can continue—mixtape culture, even the way that legal sampling has become incorporated into the musical practice. In an alternate universe it could be the case that when sampling became illegal or it became something that you were required to pay for that people would have stopped doing that and started doing something else but instead it seems that the idea of working with and transforming existing material is something that stays and it's the laws that have to continue to evolve.

- - I think the notion of the fugitive is important, especially in black culture. If there's a wall, you gotta figure out a way to get around it. I think that's probably a part of our practice.

- - That's an interesting point about the continuation of sampling legally. That approach is different than figuring out a way to get over the wall—it's just sort of doing it the right way.

- - They're using the legal system in ways that it might not have been intended for. When they made the idea of copyrighting a song, like a score for the entertainer was first invented they certainly could never have imagined that people were gonna be taking recorded snippet and try to use it to create an entirely new work where it's hard to even determine where it's derivative of the original.

- - Maybe I'm misunderstanding... Before it was illegal sampling was that: are we gonna take this untraditional way of sampling music and do something with it. And then that was made illegal and instead of taking another route and finding another interesting way of making music they continued doing that just paying for it. It didn't follow the tradition of doing something new.

- - I don't think it was that clean cut either especially in terms of hip-hop. People just started getting sued.

- - They started taking more obscure stuff.

- - There were debates about DJ Premier calling out hip-hop: "This is hip-hop. Hip-hop doesn't play by those rules." You can take whatever you want and use it.

- - He was complaining on some mixtape, saying, "Stop telling where these [samples] come from."

- - Exactly. He was like, yeah. And that when he basically made the distinction between the underground. He was like forget it then I'm just gonna go underground where everybody underground got their torches. So it's like you guys play by the rules in that. but were gonna do underground music. Take music use it how you want. I'm thinking about that because I was just listening to that, him saying that, yesterday.

- - I must have been 14 or 15 when I heard Souls of Mischief's *Taxi* remake that took the instrumental track from the *Taxi* TV show and then they created the rhyme over it about them catching taxis around their neighborhood. I had heard '*93 til infinity* and I was like oh I want to hear this song too but I couldn't find it. It's like it was a myth, nobody had it. The original taxi track they had made was on a mixtape, primarily West Coast, couldn't get it on CD. nobody in Houston owned it. And the people that owned it wouldn't share it. It was like their bragging rights: I got something you can't have. And I think that creating the laws didn't just make it financially difficult but it made it difficult for people to communicate with each other about their ideas and their innovations. If you created it could you give it to anybody? Could people absorb it? could it influence culture? And it became more difficult with that because not only could you not sell it, but when they controlled distribution routes then you couldn't distribute it. So you could make something but unless you paid them you couldn't even get it to your people on the other side of the country or your people other places through mainstream routes so it became really difficult to try and communicate those ideas because it became inaccessible without the money to pay for the legalities.

- - There's this other thing to that in the beginning of it I thought that was important because there was something that he talked about in the reading time and time again. He does this thing where he separates the culture form the people. And to me that was a powerful statement to be able to do that, to separate the culture from the people. At least this is how I read this thing. It says here," I would like to emphasize that cultural diversity its cultural ... rather than genetically instituted and reinforced..." so I was thinking, in terms of black culture, it is something that's different, that's separate, that's not of the people, that's really of the environment, right? In terms of the African American culture. If that is the case, I forget why but there were discussions about art and life at the time...

- - In the next sentence, he says that "We need to make it clear that when we speak of otherness we're not positing static ... by which otherness is maintained." I feel like this issue of our difference as African-American artists and ways that this group as a group or primarily African-American institutions the ways that those ... The way that difference is something that is maintained and not just inheres in you as an artist or as a creator. There have certainly, I think, been some differences of opinion among the group on issues relating to this because we think differently about what kind of obligation we have with relation to the particular cultural context that we've inherited and, both creatively, in our art practices what our relationship is with larger institutions, but then also socially and politically. I feel like those are extensions of conversations, even actually Lauren when you were talking about the more you learn the more there is to learn. It's so true but it's also funny how consistent the readings that we've read this fall and winter have been, how many things have come back again and again. Like Zora Neale Hurston's "Characteristics of Negro Expression"—we read that essay, then read an essay by Elizabeth Alexander that was all about that essay. It's come up over and over and over again. It's an essay that condenses a lot of the most important ongoing conversations about what it means to essentialize black identity or blackness as a set of cultural values or characteristics. [Hurston] was a trained ethnographer, anthropologist, and the essay describes a number of characteristics that she associates with the way that black people the way they use speech, the kind of stories they tell, the kind of music, the way they decorate their houses, the way they walk, anything that falls into that rubric of expression.

- - And it was a country negro. She wasn't speaking about city life. She made it real clear that your basic untutored negro you could find this in any home and they didn't have to know each other and that was the gist of the essay.

- - She was coming from her anthropological background observing this negro expression. The thing that was interesting—and I can't remember where I stood on it—the thing was we were reading it and people were saying some of that makes sense now but some of us were also saying this is a bit dated, this is not applicable, we don't relate to that text, and even found it a bit offensive, too.

- - First there was a question of... we were reading this text and she says things like we use words like chopaxe, sittingchair, cookpot and we were all reading it like, yes, umm hmm, exactly, and then at the end were like wait a minute, actually is this something that we know of indirectly or is it actually part of our experience ...

- - Or do we all just read Zora Neale Hurston?

- - Exactly, is it just that we've been reading Zora Neale Hurston for 80 years. And similarly with some of the other characteristics she describes. One of them was the interior of a house and says that black people kind of over-decorate their houses ...

- - It was about how there was no distinction between high and low.

- - Yeah, no distinction between high and low, over-beautification, everything on a doily and framed. We were reading it and it's really funny and it seemed to resonate and afterward we were like do we really feel that the African-Americans that we know are distinctive in this way or is this more a characteristic of rural culture or is it really not something that connects to us personally, it just sounds right. And it led to a larger conversation about how we evaluate the kind of claims any writer makes when they try to essentialize the qualities of a group by saying African-Americans do this. What are you really saying when you say that? how can we sue that essay? How can use those kinds of claims? What are we meant to even think about that? how are we to evaluate the truth of it? What does it mean to be true? Those kind of things.

- - At what point in time do you look at or think about stereotyping or mimicry? Especially when you think about somebody being able to identify these characteristics and put them in a package and make it commercial. And at what point in time do you think about internalizing those stereotypes and then you start saying to yourself umm hmm and then you're like wait a minute do we really do that or have I been fed that have I been reading this and been fed that so long.

- - Even in your retelling our reaction to it, I feel like that's still not doing justice to what I felt I responded to in reading some of these things. Because I think the use of the "verbage," you know, "conversate" there are certain of these imaginary words that to me it makes a lot of sense and I relate in reference to my grandparents who have a much more direct relationship to the time that Hurston was describing. it's kind of like you definitely talk about the time period B.E.T black people build a barbecue pit like this, white people build a barbecue pit like that. that's very different and that to me is the dangerous room.

- - I'm interested in ... because one of the things we looked at as we were reading it ... she talked about the black church and everybody is like yeah that's exactly how the black church is yeah this whole thing going on, the shouting over here, yeah the fans and then we realize at the end that none of had experienced it or had not in a long long long time. We were like does that church even exist anymore, so why were we doing this. But I'm interested in like alright so what is going on with black people today? What is the context? But I'm interested in whether the scope of the context has widened a little. I'm trying to fit Eminem in there. Why do we feel he's getting over on black culture. Can he be part of a context and experience such that this is his expression?

- - Every month you read about some rapper whose life is just not what he is rapping about. So if you want to talk about mimicry, aren't we kind of mimicking ourselves in some way? Hip hop is supposed to be the marker of contemporary black culture and it turns out to even be a mimicry of itself.

- - But, if we're taking stuff from other places, then does hip-hop have a legitimate response to somebody taking anything from it and when the mimicry starts happening internally. And like it was saying in the article it's not genetic. What if I'm mimicking gangsta rap, and then somebody else mimics me mimicking gangsta rap.

- - Mimicking is different though. Mimicking is brainless to me. Is there another degree of what it means to appropriate. Is that the same thing? Is stealing the same as mimicry?

- - I think there's appropriation if you're on the west coast and your appropriating West Coast styles, expressing stuff around you.

- - I don't know if that mimicry as opposed to revising. That's a big difference.

- - What about talent under duress. What about tap and—who were those two brother guys back in the day? (The Nicholas brothers). Back when it was extremely segregated and awful, right? But performing these things and still being able to come up with new [ideas]... if you're creating under this duress would that be different if you had this whole artistic ability without that racism wall drama?

- - I think that's the second album dilemma. A rap artist comes out with a first album when they're living a lifestyle, before they had the money, before the label paid them, and then they get paid they travel the world and for the past twelve months they've been in Asia and Europe and then they try to come out eighth a second album keepin' it real about what they've been doing for the last twelve months and it seems off because they don't know what they're talking about. They've been gone for twelve, twenty-four months.

- - You have to just revise. I'm thinking like a De La Soul, a Wu-Tang and all those second albums that yeah they don't have the same kind of hunger in them, right? But you still have a certain experience and you can still make art of that experience.

- - I don't see anything wrong in Eminem doing whatever he does. I think he's interesting and talented. I'm interested in him as a musician and a lyricist. But I think the frustration come out of what the music, there's a parallel with a lot of all black music. Look at free jazz and people like Albert Ayler and Coltrane and then you also look at the circumstances with hip-hop. This music came from them fighting and it was sort of a voice for voiceless and it came from a certain intense circumstance and I think that people feel that they kind of own that music because it came out of these circumstances. I think that it's evolved to another stage now where a white person can make free jazz and a white person can do hip-hop. It might have come from those circumstances but it's evolved to become something different. And I feel Eminem is authentic and I don't think it's manufactured. I think that there are interesting free jazz musicians that are white, Japanese and have put their own voice on it. It has to evolve to the next stage. We're holding on to where it originated.

- - I mean, I don't know if this is an easy way to interpret these events but just like what we just read about Tommy Dorsey or Benny Goodman becoming the King of swing, Right? Being able to capitalize off of these artistic traditions these artistic movements. I know it's a lot more complicated. I see this Eminem thing, it's more complicated, as being connected with that whole kind of history.

- - I kept asking myself questions like "are we only recognized to do something unique and original if we are always under some severe duress. We gotta be really scuffling and fighting hard to do something to be like "oh that's cutting edge." Otherwise if we're not in that vein with that tension We always be struggling. Otherwise if we are not in that kind of vien and tension ... it's distructive, I guess that's how we've always been marketed. As a way of "they'll create something outta nothing." We don't need to give nothing to them anything, they make something outta nothing. We can make somethings but these are the circumstances. And referring to that "otherness you find a peaceful space in your being even with poor circumstances. (quote from the reading) "...there was a time to sit and talk... so the skin felt powerful and human... " I kept reading to see if I could understand it.

The way [Hurston] describes how people decorate their homes and kitchens and stuff like that ... So we think, did I really see a house like that or did I just read? But we're not sure because we've bartered so much information. We don't even think about was that just fed information or else. Once you've said that I thought of music I like to listen to and words I have no connection with physically, but then they get these "touchstones." All of a sudden you get this spark in you that comes out. You can't explain it in any fashion. I've had that experience with people just sitting on the porch and not saying anything. I see that up and down this road here, people sitting on the porch not talking but there is a certain kind of connection. These almost irrelevant things but these are some of the primal things that we can all share with each other.

- - Yeah, primal. Because this is what she leads me to believe is just ... human. This is the only time these people get to be human. This moment.

- - What if those artist in those big swing jazz places still gave props to the people whose names weren't listed and were given credit for being the best swing of all time? The guys who got credit nationally. Someone had to be like "I'm down with so and so but I'm not down with that." I think it's the same way like that, (we) stopped being the center of jazz after swing music got to be so popular black people stopped being the center of it. Maybe the same thing is happening with hip hop. After hip hop reached a certain point, people weren't making music that they hoped to get signed to labels, labels just started looking for artist making music that was the music they wanted to sell.

- - For those labels, as with those jazz houses, the goal is to connect to the fun part and not look the pain that makes the work fun in the eye.

- - Doesn't that go back to, once you figure out what makes it then you can package it and give it to anybody. So then it's appropriation of memory.

- - What do you think about how they use Coltrane music to sell cars. How do you feel about that?

- - Is his family still making money?

- - All of a sudden he's put on a pedestal, but during his life he wasn't viewed that way.

- - But it introduced people, like in hip hop, who may have never heard of John Coltrane.

- - What car? It makes a difference. I think the package of Coltrane was used by white folks who wanted to be rebellious. He was packaged as the it, the music to be part of if you wanted to be loose and not like your parents.

- - Again it's a phenomenon that's not totally unique to African American culture. In the sense that The Who, which was like some radical rock band other something, is now also used to sell cars. In terms of generational shifts where the music stops being like a living thing. It kinda relates to his concern about the relationship between like action movement and nouns or objects. The music stops being like a living thing and become a sign of something. And what it is a sign of is "pastness." Coltrane becomes a sign of "jazzness." Nostalgia as a static thing. When it is used in advertisement it's not used to make action in culture.

- - It's funny, no matter where we are art we always end up talking about music. No matter what we are reading, no matter where we start, it always ends up there. It's interesting that the conversation very rarely ends up about art directly. We never talk about our own work or our own practices.

- - One of the things that you guys were talking about and it made me think about one of the things that we talk about in this group often is how we manage expectations about the kind of work we as black artist are expected to make or the kinds of references our work is expected to have.

- - It was almost kind of perceived that my work should be angry. I didn't really do anything angry at [redacted] but then you get these signals from kids... that was one of the few times I started talking about my work and before I could say something they were like hold up. And it was just perceived that my work wasn't doing what it was supposed to be doing.

- - Well it's funny because during critiques sometimes it's hard to know whether someone is responding to the work as it is or whether they are responding to whatever kind of work they would expect from me, like the kind of work that they expect you to make. I recently just a few weeks ago had a curator visit my studio and they said—they kind of was like is this work doing—I'm not sure that this work is doing what you want it to be doing. What do you think I want it to be doing and why do you think that? It's like a very weird way of phrasing this kind of evaluation, both my perceived goals as being something that is aligning or not aligning with expectations and what the work itself has to do with those goals. I know I'm not the only one who has dealt with that,it's something that we talked about a lot. It's kind of interesting. I know that [redacted] mentions it often because of her abstract work that often is interpreted metaphorically as still somehow relating to blackness or black skin, black bodies. And still, it is not to say that there are a range of references in the work, that there is a single determined meaning for the content associated with the work, but there are certain directions that people expect.

- - I had someone come to my show one time and I saw someone looking at my work and they didn't know that I was the artist. And they were looking at it, because I do sculptural work. They looked at it and they were kind of curious about it and they got really focused on it. They were moving close to it and then they saw my name. And then they started speculating, the way that they looked at was different, after they saw my name. They started speculating about who I was—the way that they looked at it was completely different. They didn't know me. They just saw "[redacted]." You know [redacted] is a pretty black name.

And they were like oh, hmm. I wonder is this a face or is, you know it immediately became images, but there are no bodies in it.

I'm conscious about my work not having anything to do with that and it may have simply because of who I am, but I am also aware of those things and we also brought up the last time we talked this idea of strategy as an artist and how are we strategic as black artists and moving our art forward in this arts world that—I don't know, maybe some else can elaborate more on—but what are the strategies that we use to move our work forward?

- - To negotiate, to navigate a context in which there are specific—it's not only like that there are specific expectations regarding what a person with a particular biography would make but also that that involves navigating the symbolic visual world of art that involves making decisions about how your work negotiates particular ideas. It was when we were talking about Martin Puryear.

- - Did you see that piece that he did for the Reagan Building?

- - Another good guy is William D. Williams.

- - William D. Williams but also Danny Johnson, I knew Danny when had a big commission at the U.N Building. He had this totem pole-less in front of the U.N. Building. He's also a musician, great saxophonist.

- - And all that goes to say: what is black art? It's every damn thing that we do.

- - How do black artists make that kind of work? Do we have to do... you know like she was saying, to continue making work and to continue getting support do you feel like there is a certain way you have to play your hand?

- - Don't be controlled by the categories that are placed on you. Get You don't want to have to jump into a category that is already created for you, and pigeonhole you because you jumped into a category... because you bit into the temptation of getting a little bitty reward. You see what I'm saying? If you can create a category then you can control the nature of the reward. They can't really place you into a category, because you're operating out of creativity. That's what creativity means: I am a category. Each individual is a category of work.

So if you are lumped into, "he's a black artist," that means somebody is going to expect everybody to do something that's related to everybody else, in order to have you in one category. That's why they come up with categories, to keep you in control. No chains. No shackles. Just a good category to stick you in.

- - I was thinking about the contrast between... I think that there is a transition—like you were talking about crit, he was talking about crit, you were talking about strategy, and ya'll were talking about government commissions... like there is this transition where other people's opinions get involved in your art making process. And I have found that—the part that I have found difficult was, I went to [redacted], I had crit at [redacted], usually I was the only black person in the room so if there was a black figure in my stuff then that was one of the context of the discussion. And so I may be around political activists, so my political activist work would have a black person in it because that's the part of political activity that I'm around. But my work is not about political activity, it's about black issues. I think it's one thing in crit, in crit I'm thing about making work. But when it comes to navigating and sells then you're thinking about selling work. If you are thinking about crit and then you get into the discussion of navigating a strategy and then you end up back in crit, I think crit can get a little confusing to me. Once you have to bring in strategy or if you bring in strategy or if you chose not to bring strategy into your art making process or into your thinking about making work, what happens then?

- - Do you really think that you cannot bring in strategy? There is no place that is untouched by the influences that affect us. The artists that we think about—it doesn't even just have to do with professional ambitions although that may be a part of it, but also it has to do with how you conceptualize a work before and as you are realizing it. There is always some bubble of thinking and rethinking and planning that's a part of most contemporary artists' process.

- - Well I think that what [redacted] was saying that he was home already so he didn't have to go nowhere. What strategy would you need to have if you didn't need to transition to somewhere else because you already were where you wanted to go.

- - Well I think the term strategy is only applied to when you see yourself as playing any sort of game. And if your posture is that there is no game for me to play, then the notion of strategy is not necessary. I think in this day in time when artists have... I don't know, I guess it depends on what you want out of your...

- - It's not that the strategy is not necessary. The strategy is self-evident. If it's visual, somebody has got to see it. It's just that simple. If it's not seen, it does not even exist.

You got to show [your work] somewhere. In this group we can develop resources that will allow you to just show what you are doing. That in itself will eliminate all of the categories.

- - The strategy has nothing to do with the center. Create your own center, let them come to you. And then your strategy is—almost in a sense—is to exist, and produce and maintain... having power over your own image.

INTROSPECTION

AFTER G.B.

Steffani Jemison

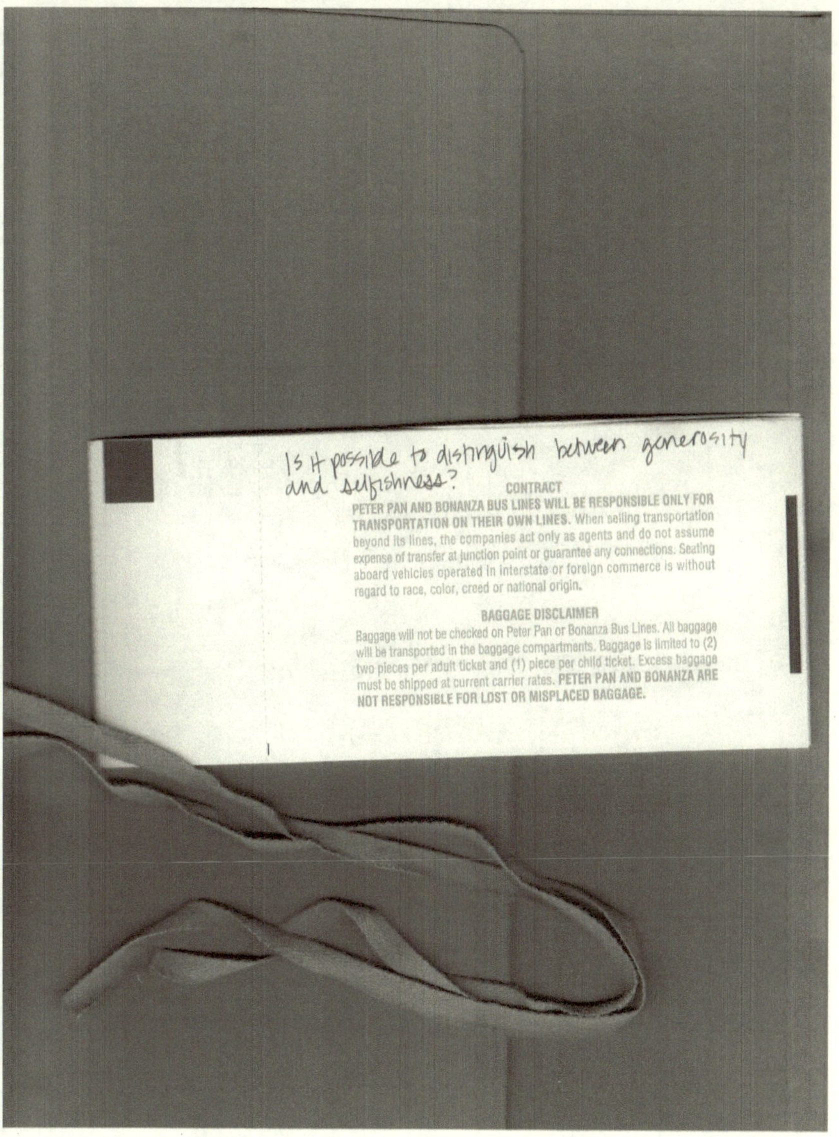
Is it possible to distinguish between generosity and selfishness?
CONTRACT
PETER PAN AND BONANZA BUS LINES WILL BE RESPONSIBLE ONLY FOR TRANSPORTATION ON THEIR OWN LINES. When selling transportation beyond its lines, the companies act only as agents and do not assume expense of transfer at junction point or guarantee any connections. Seating aboard vehicles operated in interstate or foreign commerce is without regard to race, color, creed or national origin.
BAGGAGE DISCLAIMER
Baggage will not be checked on Peter Pan or Bonanza Bus Lines. All baggage will be transported in the baggage compartments. Baggage is limited to (2) two pieces per adult ticket and (1) piece per child ticket. Excess baggage must be shipped at current carrier rates. PETER PAN AND BONANZA ARE NOT RESPONSIBLE FOR LOST OR MISPLACED BAGGAGE.

A5
PRESORTED AUTO
FIRST-CLASS MAIL
U.S. POSTAGE PAID
AETNA
30329
Important Information Enclosed
IS INTROSPECTION
SELFISH?
GBP-GP1 11225

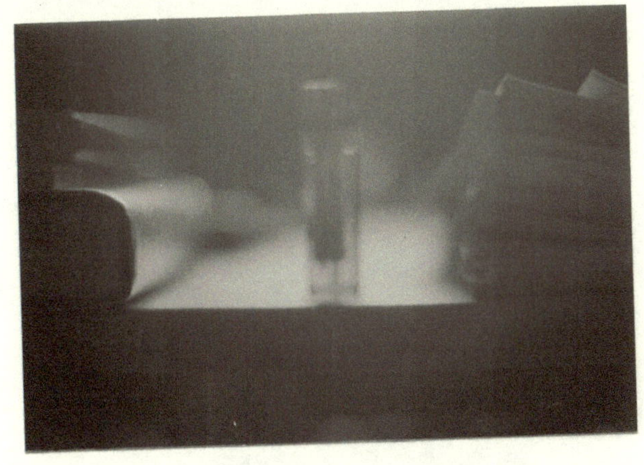

Is selflessness
possible?
achievable?
desirable?

how can our obligations help us reach our ideals?

citibank®

1398 FULTON ST, BROOKLYN, NY

DATE 10-26-2011
TIME 15:04
ATM ID 000005293
CARD XXXXXXXXXXXX6590

Experience JAY-Z and Kanye West on the WATCH THE THRONE tour!
As a Citibank® Debit MasterCard® customer, you can get special access to purchase Citi Preferred tickets*.
Get details at citiprivatepass.com.
*All dates subject to change.
Tickets subject to availability.

CHECK DEPOSIT $ 1,400.00
To: Basic Checking
XXXXX521

how can I focus
exclusively on
possibilities?

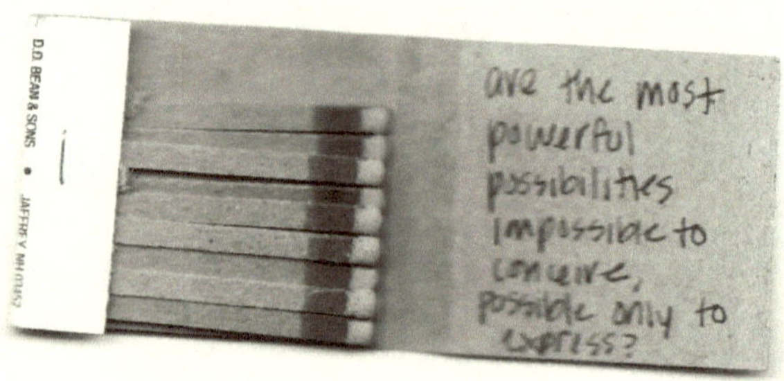
D.D. BEAN & SONS • JAFFREY NH
are the most
powerful
possibilities
impossible to
conceive,
possible only to
express?

Is power merely a metaphor, or is it a fact, or is it a force?

of a subject through firsthand experience. By the terms of this model, whether traveling

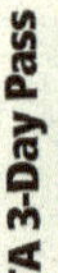
EDM 3672-8 9876543210
1431455678
USE BY 03/01/12P 05:54PM 18JUN11
Is anyone truly power less??
CTA 3-Day Pass
• Valid for unlimited rides on CTA for 72 hours from date & time of first use and no value can be added to pass
• Pass cannot be shared, and must be used by the expiration date shown
• Pass cannot be replaced, refunded or redeemed for cash
• Passes cannot be used more than once on the same bus or at same rail station in any given 30 minute period
Travel Information: (312) 836-7000
Customer Service: 1-888-YOUR-CTA
transitchicago.com
REGULATIONS: Use of the 3-Day Pass is subject to all applicable tariffs, terms, conditions, rules, regulations, policies and procedures CTA may in its discretion adopt from time to time. CTA expressly reserves the right to make changes to the afore-mentioned at any time without advance notice.
© 2009 CTA

"[This] new biography of Indian national-
ist hero Subhas Chandra Bose could help
resuscitate the leader's troubled reputation
outside of India. . . Bose's life is an action-
packed thriller tailor-made for biographical
treatment."

—Tom Wright, *Wall Street Journal blog*

Belknap Press / new in cloth / $35.00

number of sites and has shaped this
diverse evidence into a smart and
plausible narrative."

—Jeffrey Collins, *Wall Street Journal*

"A fascinating look back through our
intellectual history and an excellent view
of the foundations of modern populism."

—Christopher Holden, *PopMatters*

New in cloth / $29.95

reform . . . It's the stories in [Garrett's] book
that stick in the memory. One can only hope
that they will mobilize a broad range of
citizens, liberal and conservative, to demand
legislative and judicial reforms."

—Jeffrey Rosen, *New York Times*

New in cloth / $39.95

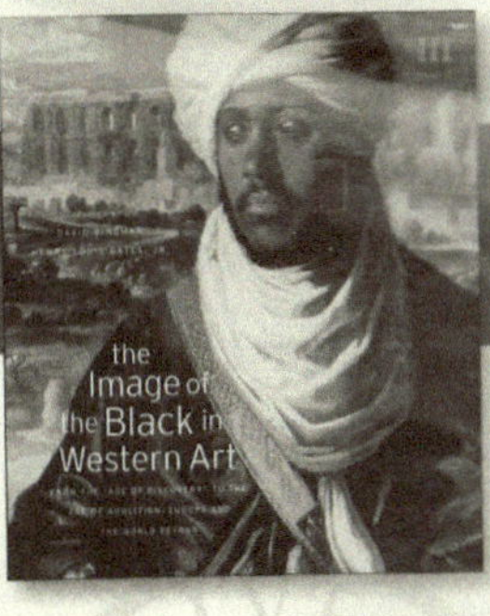

HARVARD UNIVERSITY PRESS
WWW.HUP.HARVARD.EDU
BLOG: HARVARDPRESS.TYPEPAD.COM
TEL: 800.495.1619

Is power a property of people?

ELD

s and the

s is one of the most dangerous
ly a steady, steely academic
wide open, pencil to the metal,
provocative and lively collection."

Book Review

THE IMAGE OF THE BLACK IN WESTERN ART

Volume III: From the "Age of Discovery" to the Age of Abolition, Part 2: Europe and the World Beyond

EDITED BY DAVID BINDMAN & HENRY LOUIS GATES, JR.

"In addition to being an indispensable guide to the evolving meanings of racial difference, these dazzling volumes filled with extraordinary images and rich arguments contribute to an alternative history of the Western world. An invaluable gift for both specialists and general readers."

—Paul Gilroy

Belknap Press / new in cloth / $95.00
www.imageoftheblack.com/

heavy water blues

1967

The radio is teaching my goldfish Jujutsu
I am in love with a skindiver who sleeps underwater,
My neighbors are drunken linguists, & I speak butterfly,
Consolidated Edison is threatening to cut off my brain,
The postman keeps putting sex in my mailbox,
My mirror died, & can't tell if i still reflect,
I put my eyes on a diet, my tears are gaining too much weight.

I crossed the desert in a taxicab
only to be locked in a pyramid
With the face of a dog
on my breath

I went to a masquerade
Disguised as myself
Not one of my friends
Recognized

I dreamed I went to John Mitchell's poetry party
in my maidenform brain

Put the silver in the barbeque pit
The Chinese are attacking with nuclear
Restaurants

The radio is teaching my goldfish Ju Jutsu
My old lady has taken up skin diving & sleeps underwater

Is it possible for power to be lost, or is it only transferred? Does it tranfer consistently, like heat transfers from hot air to cool air, in search of equilibrium? or does it transfer consistently, like my trash transfers to the landfill, away from the individual and toward the mass?

INDEX
With and for: "Black Mo'nin'," by Fred Moten*
by Regina Agu

* Moten, Fred. "Black Mo'nin'." Eng and Kazanjian, *Loss: The Politics of Mourning.* Berkeley: University of California Press, 2003. 59–76

The tilde (~) stands for the head-word in a given entry.
Links to terms listed elsewhere in this index are shown in **bold face.**

—C—

—D—

—E—

—R—

—S—

—U—

—V—

—W—

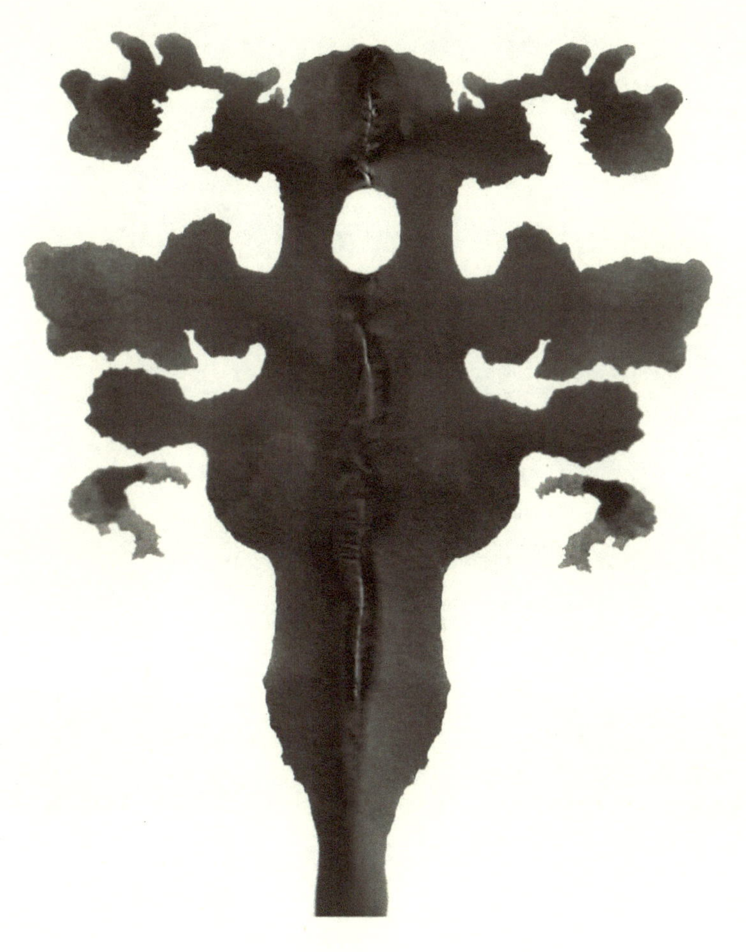

Book Club is a reading group and think tank incubated by Project Row Houses in Houston, Texas. The group convenes biweekly to investigate progressive, experimental, and provocative texts, with a particular focus on hard-to-find work by black authors.

Book Club Book is a collection of emails, dialogues, poems, questions, fiction, and memoranda by artists and writers involved with Book Club in 2010-2011. Book Club Book contributors include:

Regina Agu
Nathaniel Donnett
Quincy Flowers
Egie Ighile
Lauren Kelley
Steffani Jemison
Otabenga Jones & Associates
Ayanna Jolivet McCloud
Massa Lemu
Bert Long
Jesse Lott
Rick Lowe
Mo Roberts
Bert Samples
George Smith
Kaneem Smith
M'kina Tapscott
Michael Kahlil Taylor

Illustrations, pp. 14, 16, 19: Otabenga Jones & Associates
Photograph, p. 26: Quincy Flowers
Illustrations pp. 11, 45, 81, 105, 129, 167: Nathaniel Donnett
Photographs, pp. 147, 148, 149, 150, 151, 152, 152, 154, 155, 156: Steffani Jemison
Photographs, pp. 49, 74: Bert Long

ISBN: 978-0-9833815-2-5

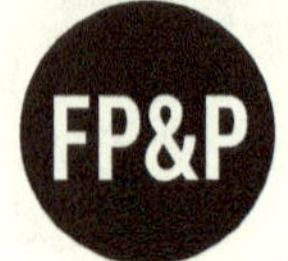

future plan and program

Future Plan and Program
http://futureplanandprogram.com

Please direct inquiries to:
thefuture@futureplanandprogram.com

Series editor: Steffani Jemison
Series designer: Sebastian Civarolo

Future Plan and Program was incubated in 2010-2011 by Project Row Houses.

Acknowledgements: Danielle Burns, Justin Cavin, Aisen Chacin, Ashley Clemmer-Hoffman, Cheryl Flores, Quincy Flowers, Hannah Ireland, Philip Jemison, Steven Jemison, Rick Lowe, Jasmine Jamillah Mahmoud, Phyllis McCallum, Solkem N'Gangbet, Michael Peranteau, Nikki Pressley, Linda Shearer, Martine Syms, Michael Kahlil Taylor, and Julie Thomson.

Future Plan and Program was generously funded in part by the following individuals: Kerry Inman & Denby Auble, John Roberson & John Blackmon, Danielle Antoinette Burns, Justin Cavin, Jereann Chaney, Melody Clark, Ashley Clemmer Hoffman & Brendan Hoffman, Phyllis L. McCallum and Steven Jemison, Joey Romano & Nicole Laurent, Victoria Thomas McGhee, Scott Sawyer & Michael Peranteau, Gregory & Diane Schultz, Leigh & Reggie Smith, and Rebecca Trahan. Special thanks to Jill Whitten & Robert Proctor.

Funding for Steffani Jemison's residency at Project Row Houses was provided by: The National Endowment for the Arts, the City of Houston through the Houston Arts Alliance, Houston Endowment Inc., The Brown Foundation, The Kresge Foundation, The Andy Warhol Foundation for the Visual Arts, and the Texas Commission on the Arts. Steffani Jemison's residency was part of a collaboration with the Core Program at the Glassell School of Art of the Museum of Fine Arts Houston.

www.ingramcontent.com/pod-product-compliance
Lightning Source LLC
LaVergne TN
LVHW050959080826
845145LV00009B/2356

9780983381525